ROMMEL'S AFRIKA KORPS IN COLOUR

ALSO BY ANTHONY TUCKER-JONES

Life and Death on the Eastern Front:
Unique Colour Photographs from the Second World War
Kursk 1943: Hitler's Bitter Harvest
Slaughter on the Eastern Front: Hitler and Stalin's War 1941–1945
Stalin's Revenge: Operation Bagration and the Annihilation of Army Group Centre
Stalin's Armour 1941–1945: Soviet Tanks at War

IMAGES OF WAR
Armoured Warfare on the Eastern Front
Armoured Warfare and Hitler's Allies 1941–1945
Tank Wrecks of the Eastern Front 1941–1945
The Battle for Budapest 1944–1945
The Battle for the Caucasus 1942–1943
The Battle for the Crimea 1941–1944
The Battle for Kharkov 1941–1943
The Battle for Warsaw 1939–1945
The Eastern Front Air War 1941–1945

ROMMEL'S AFRIKA KORPS IN COLOUR

Rare German Photographs from the Second World War

TEXT BY ANTHONY TUCKER-JONES
IMAGES FROM THE PIXPAST ARCHIVE

Greenhill
Books

The publisher would like to thank Peter Reisch for generously permitting the inclusion of his father Max Reisch's rare colour photo slides alongside Pixpast's collection.

Ian Spring: I would like to take this opportunity to thank my parents Declan and Sylvia for their life-long support of my hobby. Also to the countless families of Second World War veterans that have donated their wartime colour slides to my archive. Finally a big thank you to my beautiful little daughter Fiona Francis Spring for helping put in the photo slides in the scanner to help daddy :)

Rommel's Afrika Korps in Colour: Rare German Photographs from the Second World War

Greenhill
Books

First published in 2023
by Greenhill Books, Lionel Leventhal Ltd
c/o Pen & Sword Books Ltd,
George House, Unit 12 & 13, Beevor Street, Off Pontefract Road, Barnsley, South Yorkshire S71 1HN
For more information on our books, please visit
www.greenhillbooks.com, email contact@greenhillbooks.com
or write to us at the above address.

CIP data records for this title are available from the British Library
ISBN 978-1-78438-879-9
Typeset and designed by www.mousematdesign.com
Printed and bound in India by Replika Press Pvt. Ltd.

FSC
www.fsc.org
MIX
Paper from responsible sources
FSC® C016779

Contents

Introduction: The 'Desert Fox'

FIELD MARSHAL ERWIN ROMMEL, both during the Second World War and after, was seen as a mythic bogeyman who ran circles around the British military in North Africa. Such was his wily reputation that he became known as the 'Desert Fox'. In part his legend was a result of him facing down the British 8th Army – his fame in particular rivalling that of his counterpart Field Marshal Bernard Montgomery.

However, Rommel's remarkable exploits were much wider than that. In 1940, at the head of the 7th Panzer Division during the invasion of France, he swiftly cut through French defences. He also dramatically thwarted a British armoured counterattack at Arras. The speed of his advance was such that his command was nicknamed the 'Ghost Division'. In 1943, after the Axis defeat in North Africa and in the wake of Benito Mussolini's fall from power,

Above: Rommel, stood second from the right, has just given a film interview to the cine-cameraman on the left somewhere in Tunisia in 1942 for *Die Deutsche Wochenschau* – the *German Weekly Review* – which was broadcast in German cinemas. Rommel's media profile was greatly assisted by the presence on his staff of Lieutenant Alfred-Ingemar Berndt, a Deputy Reich Press Chief from the Propaganda Ministry, ensuring he was a favourite of the Nazi Propaganda Minister Joseph Goebbels.

Opposite: Erwin Rommel, again on the right, was the master of the photo opportunity. He was supremely photogenic and was photographed on an almost daily basis in North Africa. Seen here conferring with an Italian colonel, he had little time for his Axis allies. Although subordinate to the Italian chain of command, he acted as if he was the senior partner. On occasions Italian troops showed great courage and tenacity, but on the whole Rommel saw the Italian military more of a hindrance than a help.

PK-reporter or Kriegsberichter Fritz Moosmüller, smoking his pipe, seated on his trusted Kübelwagen somewhere in North Africa. The yellow PK on the front left-hand mudguard stands for Propaganda Kompanie, part of the Wehrmacht's Propaganda troops. They came under Oberkommando der Wehrmacht (OKW), or High Command Armed Forces, and the Nazi Propaganda Ministry.

Rommel orchestrated the successful occupation of northern Italy. This prolonged the war by ensuring the Allies became bogged down with the Italian campaign.

Rommel was then sent to France to take charge of Army Group B and to shake up German defences in Normandy. Constantly on the move, he was a human whirlwind exhorting his generals to do better. Many historians have speculated that the battle of Normandy might have gone better for Hitler if Rommel had been given a free hand and not been wounded and hospitalised. Subsequently Rommel's implication in the 20 July 1944 bomb plot to kill Hitler resulted in him being forced to commit suicide on 14 October that year in order to save his wife and son.

In the post-war years men who had served under Rommel began to sing his praises. Notably Lieutenant Heinz Werner Schmidt, who had been on Rommel's staff, published his memoir, *With Rommel in the Desert*, in 1951. Schmidt was highly impressed by Rommel's go-getting and risk-taking attitude. Indeed, the Field Marshal's mantra had always been to take the battle to the enemy. When Rommel had first arrived in Tripoli in early 1941, Hitler instructed him to wait until his forces were fully assembled before taking action. Rommel ignored this and immediately attacked the British, rolling them out of Libya and back to the Egyptian frontier.

Luftwaffe Kriegsberichter Otto Vieth covered the war in the Mediterranean. He regularly took photographs for the Luftwaffe's propaganda magazine *Der Adler*. His camera is sporting an extended lens, presumably for aerial work.

Kriegsberichter Moosmüller enjoying a glass of wine on a terrace overlooking Tunis in Tunisia. He took delight in photographing the assorted colonial forces deployed in North Africa.

Rommel's reputation was further enhanced when his diaries and letters, edited by Basil Liddell Hart, were published as *The Rommel Papers* in 1953. This was done with the full cooperation of his wife Lucie-Maria, his son Manfred and General Fritz Bayerlein, who as a colonel had served as Rommel's chief of staff in North Africa. This book confirmed that Rommel was a great tactical and strategic thinker, especially in North Africa. Ironically, his greatest obstacle was not Montgomery, but Hitler, who constantly refused to let him take the initiative or to give him the resources he needed to win.

This war photographer, with his Leica camera round his neck, served in Italy. On the orders of Joseph Goebbels, the Nazi Propaganda Minister, the Propaganda Kompanien were only authorised to use German-made cameras.

The Rommel Papers also showed Rommel in a very human light. He regularly wrote to his wife and son to reassure them that he was safe, and he worried about the well-being of his men. The terrible stresses and strains of command resulted in him continually suffering from ill health. His illness was in fact often caused by his insistence that he live off field rations like his men. His batman Lance Corporal Herbert Günther tried his best to ensure that Rommel ate well, but it was not always easy. In desperate need of a rest in August 1942, Rommel suggested that General Heinz Guderian, the creator of Germany's Panzer-truppen, replace him – but Hitler refused. Rommel, though, proved more resilient than most. In January 1942 he noted, 'I'll soon be the only one of the German officers who's seen the whole thing through from start to finish.'

Rommel's ill health may partially account for his often abrasive dealings with his commanders. He was frequently at loggerheads with his staff and subordinates. 'Rommel was not an easy man to serve; he spared those around him as little as he spared himself,' recalled Friedrich von Mellenthin, who as a major was on his staff. Luftwaffe General Stefan Fröhlich, the Fliegerführer Afrika, experienced, as did many others, a turbulent relationship with Rommel. Luftwaffe Field Marshal Albert Kesselring, the German Commander-in-Chief South, noted that Rommel did not get on well with Marshal Ettore Bastico, the Italian governor general in Libya. Technically Rommel was subordinate to the Italian chain of command, but in reality he took little notice of it. Interestingly, Kesselring was very circumspect in his own memoirs when commenting on Rommel.

Despite his Spartan lifestyle and exacting standards, Rommel did have a sense of humour. When presented with two chickens he kept them as mascots that accompanied him on the road. He also had a fondness for music. 'He learnt to play the violin,' recalled Manfred Rommel, 'and though he believed that this tuition was successful, this view was not shared by those who had to listen.'

The Deutsches Afrika Korps

The designation Deutsches Afrika Korps (DAK), or German Africa Corps, although often used as a blanket term for all German forces in North Africa, only really applied to the 5th Light Division (subsequently renamed 21st Panzer Division) and the 15th Panzer Division, which were the very first German units to land in Tripoli, plus the 90th Light Division, which was initially known as Division zbV Afrika. 'The Afrika Korps followed Rommel wherever he led, however hard he drove them,' wrote von Mellenthin, 'it was always the same Afrika Korps with the same three divisions at Sidi Rezegh, at Agedabia, at Knightsbridge, and at El Alamein.' They also thought greatly of Colonel Fritz Bayerlein who served as their chief of staff. 'The Afrika Korps has a particularly high regard for him and has much to thank him for,' noted Rommel.

All other formations, including the German 19th Flak Division, 164th Light Division, Ramcke Parachute Brigade plus the Italian armoured and motorised divisions, first came under Panzer Group Afrika, then Panzer Army Afrika in August 1941 and January 1942 respectively. Rommel commanded both the latter, while Generals Ludwig Crüwell, Walther Nehring and Hans-Jürgen von Arnim were the successive leaders of the Afrika Korps. The

Enjoying the view. Two PK-reporters languishing against their captured British Army sedan pose for a colleague. On the left is a grinning Moosmüller – he grew a beard in 1942. Propaganda Kompanien were deployed throughout the Mediterranean to record and report on the Wehrmacht's exploits.

Another PK-reporter with camera. Both men are wearing the standard German Army tropical uniform and appear to be waiting for something, possibly a passing convoy.

The two Germans go for a stroll up the hill. The locals seem completely indifferent to their presence.

Italian divisions were directed by the Italian 10th, 20th and 21st Corps. In October 1942 the army was renamed the Deutsche-Italienische Panzer Army to better reflect its composition. In February 1943 the combined Axis forces were known as Army Group Afrika and comprised the Italian 1st Army and the German 5th Panzer Army. The final Afrika Korps battle group under the command of Colonel Irkens consisted of elements of the 5th and 8th Panzer Regiments, as well as units from the 7th Panzer Regiment belonging to the 10th Panzer Division.

Annoyingly for Rommel, the Luftwaffe units deployed to Libya were not subordinate to the Afrika Korps. Instead the Fliegerführer Afrika, Luftwaffe General Fröhlich, and his successors answered directly to Field Marshal Kesselring who as Commander-in-Chief South was responsible for the whole of the Mediterranean and North Africa. In this role Kesselring was Rommel's immediate boss. Nonetheless, the Luftwaffe's dive-bombers acted as Rommel's flying artillery on numerous occasions, and Rommel does seem to have worked well with Air Marshal Hoffman von Waldau, Air Officer Commander-in-Chief Afrika, especially when it came to taking Tobruk. However, even von Waldau felt compelled to complain to Kesselring when he felt his air attacks on Bir Hacheim were not being adequately protected by Rommel's flak units. This was because the aircraft were being used in an anti-tank role.

Bemused locals watch the German convoy pass by, while a young lad in the foreground offers the cameraman a loaf of bread – selling bread to the soldiers.

Inevitably the Germans acted like tourists – as did many Europeans posted to North Africa. They were fascinated by the extensive Roman ruins as well as Arab and Berber culture. The architecture of this mosque made for a good shot.

Operation *Sunflower*

The Deutsches Afrika Korps first came into being with Operation *Sunflower. Sonnenblume* or *Sunflower* was authorised by Hitler four days before the humiliating surrender of the Italian 10th Army at Beda Fomm on 7 February 1941 in the eastern Libyan province of Cyrenaica. The previous month, he had announced that he was prepared to assist Mussolini's war effort by providing some forces to help defend Libya's western province Tripolitania when it became apparent that the Italians were incapable of fending off Major General O'Connor's British Western Desert Force in Cyrenaica. Hitler only agreed to commit two panzer divisions if the Italians withdrew no further than Sirte on the Gulf of Sirte, which lay between Tripoli and El Aghelia. If the Italians continued to withdraw, it seemed certain the Libyan capital Tripoli would be lost.

On 8 February 1941 a small advance party of what became the DAK arrived in the Italian port of Naples. Three days later they landed in Tripoli. The armoured cars of the 3rd Reconnaissance Battalion, 5th Light Division, landed on 14 February and were rushed up to Sirte. Not long afterwards two tank battalions of the 5th Panzer Regiment arrived. Their journey had not been without mishap. In Naples a cargo vessel caught fire and sank, taking with it thirteen panzers. Replacements did not reach the 5th Panzer Regiment until the end of April 1941. The 8th Panzer Regiment belonging to the 15th Panzer Division was shipped in three convoys to Tripoli between 25 April and 6 May 1941. Once his men were ashore, Rommel insisted on holding a parade for the benefit of local Italian military and political officials. His men, dressed in their new tropical topees, tunics, trousers and knee-length desert boots, looked suitably impressive.

Thanks to Rommel's impetuousness, the defensive nature of Operation *Sunflower* did not last long. Even though he was supposed to be assembling a blocking force, Rommel decided that the best way to defend Tripolitania was by launching an eastward offensive from Sirte. This would secure the marshy area 20 miles west of El Aghelia and would provide an ideal defensive position. Meeting no British resistance, the 5th Light Division moved up to this area and, along with the Italian Ariete Armoured Division, set about establishing their defences.

Rommel was delighted when intelligence informed him that most of the Western Desert Force had withdrawn to Egypt, leaving the weak British 2nd Armoured Division, Australian 9th Division and the Indian 3rd Motorised Brigade to hold Cyrenaica. He suggested to General Italo Gariboldi, his immediate Italian superior, that they launch an attack before the onset of the summer weather in May. Gariboldi agreed and the pair were given permission to retake Cyrenaica and push into Egypt. A long-term goal was to seize the Suez Canal.

The Axis attack was launched on 24 March 1941 when Rommel seized El Aghelia ready for a push forward by the 5th Light Division as well as the Italian Ariete and Brescia Divisions. These forces were later to be reinforced by elements of the 15th Panzer Division and the Italian Trento Division. The British, who had denuded their forces in North Africa in order to send an expeditionary force to Greece, were thrown back in disarray. On 11 April 1941 Rommel cut off the Australian 9th Division in the port of Tobruk and by the end of the month had reached the Halfaya Pass on Egypt's western border, having liberated Cyrenaica. From this point on the Axis and British armies would fight a war back and forth along the North African coast until Rommel's defeat at El Alamein in November 1942.

A walk through history. A German photographer strolls among the ruins of a Roman amphitheatre with his camera slung over his shoulder. Despite their tourism, the PK-reporters shared the hardships of the front-line troops.

The Desert War

The vast deserts of Egypt and Libya were on the whole good tank country, although they were exposed to shelling and air attack. There were few major towns and cities – the ones that existed were largely confined to the coast. This meant that there were far fewer civilians to get caught in the crossfire or be swept up in atrocities. Rommel chose to ignore Italian crimes and the carrying out of Nazi policies behind the lines. The Libyans were granted Italian nationality in 1939 but this did little to encourage them to support the Italian or German war effort in North Africa. The locals largely treated the war with indifference, apart from the two short-lived Libyan divisions conscripted by the Italians. These formed part of the Royal Corps of Libyan Troops and both were lost resisting the British Operation *Compass* in 1941–42. Attempts by the Germans to appeal to Arab nationalism were not successful, apart from the Deutsch-Arabische Truppen who served with the 5th Panzer Army in Tunisia. Few of them saw combat.

The Western Desert runs from Gazala in Libya almost 400 miles east to El Alamein in Egypt. It extends south 150 miles to the oases of Jarabub and Siwa. In Cyrenaica the Via Balbia road ran east from El Aghelia via Mersa Brega up the coastal outcrop of the Jebel Akhdar to Benghazi, north to Brace and eastward through Derna, Gazala, Tobruk, finally reaching Bardia near the Egyptian border. In Egypt the coastal road passed through Sollum, Sidi Barrani, Mersa Matruh, El Alamein and on to Cairo. It was between El Aghelia and El Alamein that the key battles between the Afrika Korps and the British 8th Army were fought. El Alamein was protected by the Mediterranean Sea to the north and the impassable Qattara Depression to the south. This meant the fighting for El Alamein was confined to a relatively narrow strip of firm ground.

The air and maritime war greatly impacted on the land fighting in North Africa. Axis air and naval forces fought running battles with the RAF and Royal Navy. The latter sought to escort convoys to Malta and Alexandria while also trying to cut Rommel's supply routes from Italy. The British presence on Malta created an unwelcome choke point in the Axis lines of communication in the middle of the Mediterranean. The vast distances along the coast meant that the logistics war became a major preoccupation for both sides. This is what made the port of Tobruk so vital to both sides; the more ground a victor gained, the longer the lines of communication became. Time and time again Rommel fought his way as far forward as possible, only to run out of fuel and men. The fighting was typically restricted to daytime and usually only lasted three to four hours a day. Ultimately British aircraft and submarines operating from Malta would help throttle Rommel's supplies.

The Kriegsberichter and Deputy Reichspressechef

Rommel's daring exploits in North Africa made him a darling of the Nazi Propaganda Ministry. He and his men were constantly photographed and there was extensive news coverage in German newspapers and military publications such as *Der Adler*, *Die Wehrmacht* and *Signal*. Their every move was followed closely by a team of combat reporters from the military's Propaganda Kompanien, known as PK-reporters or Kriegsberichter. These reporters answered not only to the military but also to Joseph Goebbels's Propaganda Ministry. Rommel regularly featured on the cover of *Die Wehrmacht* and *Signal*.

Still life. Crates of corned beef from Argentina, Brazil and Uruguay captured from the British. The photographer decided to make a small pyramid out of the spilt cans. The brands include Devon, Fray Bentos and Swift. Corned beef, a staple of the British armed forces in North Africa, was dubbed by the troops 'desert chicken'.

Among the Kriegsberichter who recorded Rommel's operations were photographers Eric Borchert and Hanns Gert von Esebeck and cine-cameraman Hans Ertl. Ertl, who had worked on Nazi propaganda films with director Leni Riefenstahl, gained a reputation as 'Rommel's photographer'. Borchert was killed in action at Tobruk in early 1942. Other PK-reporters included Fritz Moosmüller, who covered the fighting in Tunisia, and Otto Vieth, who served with the Luftwaffe, photographing its war effort in the Mediterranean and Tunisia. Both men regularly took photos while off duty and indeed were regularly photographed themselves. Before his arrival in North Africa, Vieth had covered the 1942 summer campaign on the Eastern Front with his trusty Leica III camera.

Rommel was lucky because he had a close publicity ally who fought his corner with both Goebbels and Hitler. Attached to his staff was Lieutenant Alfred-Ingemar Berndt, a Deputy Reichspressechef (Deputy Reich Press Chief) from the Propaganda Ministry who served Rommel as an aide-de-camp. Lieutenant Heinz Schmidt noted, 'This burly man with his great bowed head often reminded me of a bear.' Schmidt added, 'Although he wore the uniform of an ordinary lieutenant, he liked to give the impression that he was still an influential figure in the Ministry of Propaganda.'

Being in his mid-thirties, Berndt was rather old to be just a lieutenant, but he had no scruples about using his connections to benefit Rommel and himself. Rommel described Berndt as 'a man with a very persuasive tongue'. Kesselring rather scathingly called him 'Rommel's mouthpiece'. He acted as Rommel's personal emissary with Goebbels and Hitler as well as his eyes and ears in meetings with senior commanders. Rommel also deployed

Another still life. German tropical uniform, sun helmet and boots laid out on some rocks. Its owner, whose legs can be seen on the left, is about to go for a swim in the Mediterranean Sea.

Berndt to the front numerous times to assess the situation and get things moving. On at least one occasion he took charge of some anti-tank guns and drove off a British tank attack. Berndt seems to have enjoyed these roles and the opportunities they presented. As a result, he looked up to Rommel and repaid him with loyalty. Rommel trusted him so much that on occasions he delegated Berndt to write to his wife on his behalf.

Lieutenant Schmidt, who got to know Berndt, recalled:

> I saw then that he was contributing more than most people realised to the steadily growing Rommel legend. He took every opportunity of arranging photographs to be taken of the 'Desert Fox,' for publication at home and in neutral countries. Rommel himself, as war correspondents will testify, readily allowed himself to be photographed. I noticed that he often deliberately fell into a pose that would make the photographer's task easier and more effective.

The Kriegsberichter answered to Berndt. Schmidt confirmed that 'Ertl, a typical mountaineer-type of a man, who was equipped with a movie camera … took his instructions about publicising Rommel from Berndt.' Images of Rommel, his sand goggles perched on his officer's cap, such as the one of him standing up in his staff car while on patrol with the 15th Panzer Division, became iconic. In fact, the goggles were not particular to North Africa, as he had been photographed wearing a pair at St Valery-en-Caux in France in 1940. However, the ones he used in North Africa had been captured from the British at Mechili along with a British command vehicle which he redeployed and dubbed a Mammoth.

Ordinary soldiers also wanted to photograph their commander. Rommel's adjutant Major Hans-Joachim Schraepler recalled a particularly chaotic incident at Derna on 9 June 1941: 'Hundreds of German and Italian soldiers surrounded our car,' he wrote, 'directed dozens of cameras on the general … Rommel had to struggle very hard to escape the undisciplined soldier-photographers.' The crowd only thinned out when a British bomber passed overhead.

Rommel flew to Berlin in September 1942 and despite his defeat at Alam Halfa was given a hero's welcome. With Goebbels and Berndt at his side, he met Hitler and the press and attended a Nazi rally. In early November 1942 he sent Berndt to see Hitler to warn him that the war in North Africa 'was probably lost'. After his defeat at El Alamein, Rommel knew that at best retreating might save his army; Hitler's response was that he must stand firm. Once more an exhausted Rommel stood up to Hitler and conducted a highly disciplined fighting withdrawal back towards Tripoli and ultimately the Tunisian border.

Berndt could have been a hostile Nazi spy but he greatly admired Rommel, and his glowing reports ensured that Goebbels did as well. It was in part Goebbels's support that ensured Rommel got another job after the Axis defeat in Tunisia in May 1943. Putting the 'Desert Fox' in charge of Hitler's Atlantic Wall defences was inevitably seen as a coup for Nazi propaganda and a great morale booster.

Rommel was an enthusiastic chronicler of his own military career using photography. He had bought himself a Leica camera in 1939 and carried it everywhere as he drove through France the following year. He took many thousands of photos and colour slides, also regularly using a Leica which Goebbels had given him. He would frequently task his aide-de-camp to take shots of him and his other staff officers.

This Remarkable Collection

This selection of incredible colour images is courtesy of the superlative Pixpast Archive created by Ian Spring. He has painstakingly built up a collection of over 30,000 German Agfacolor slides. While many of them were taken by Kriegsberichter for propaganda purposes, shots were also often taken during more unguarded moments and show what everyday life was like for German soldiers sent to Libya, Egypt and Tunisia. These images vividly depict German troops not only on the front line, but also behind the lines relaxing and interacting with the civilian population and local colonial units. The work of professionals such as Fritz Moosmüller and Otto Vieth often captured moments of levity and these feature throughout.

The vibrancy of the colours makes the images so much more intimate and gives them a sense of immediacy. German soldiers in North Africa were photographed in a huge variety of uniforms consisting of shirts, jackets, riding breeches or jodhpurs, trousers and shorts of various length. Headgear comprised the tropical sun helmet or – at least initially (it was soon largely abandoned as impractical) – officer's cap, *Bergmütze* or peaked field cap, the *Feldmütze* or side cap and steel helmet. These colour photographs show that there was little standardisation in tropical uniform colours. They ranged from brown, orangey-sand, sage green, sand and even off-white. This was in part due to the dyes employed, but also a result of fading after continual washing and the bleaching effect of the sunshine. The Agfacolor film picks up all these glorious variations and shows individuals sporting a multitude of different uniform colours. On all Agfacolor packaging, it said Agfacolor was not intended for hot climates. This led to a lot of Agfacolor not being used in Africa and what was used was often badly damaged from the excessive cold and heat, making original colour photos from the African campaign especially rare.

Life and Death in North Africa

The fighting in North Africa was completely different to that on the Eastern and Western fronts thanks to the geography and the climate. During the summer months the temperature could reach 110 degrees in the shade, meaning that water was a priority; heatstroke, sunburn and dehydration awaited the unprepared. At night it remained atrociously hot, making it difficult to sleep. In contrast Rommel wrote that during the winter, 'The nights are bitterly cold and damp.' Grit and flies covered everything and clogged engines. The constant inhalation of sand created respiratory problems. Eating and drinking often involved swallowing grit, dust and files, causing stomach ailments. Likewise, the sand irritated the eyes, as did the glare of the sun. When conditions were particularly bad, officers and men wore scarves over their mouths and nostrils; to protect their eyes, they used sand goggles and sunglasses. Sand flies, fleas and mosquitoes made life a misery by constantly biting exposed flesh. There were many other creepy-crawlies too; Rommel resorted to standing the legs of his bed in water-filled tins to keep them at bay.

During the day and at night when the Axis armoured columns were not on the move, they had to form a desert laager, like an old-fashioned Wild West wagon circle, to provide all-round defence on the exposed terrain. Any movement threw up huge clouds of dust which invited shelling or bombing. This danger meant that when they were on the move, vehicles had to travel very widely dispersed and even though this made them less of a target, they were still at risk of running into soft ground or minefields. Despite all this, General Wilhelm Ritter von Thoma, who was captured in North Africa, far preferred the terrain to the mud and swamps of the Eastern Front. 'Africa was paradise in comparison,' he said. 'Tank troops who had been in Russia found it easy to adapt themselves to the African conditions.'

Rommel's Afrika Korps fought to the very last. Its original units including the 15th and 21st Panzer Divisions were both lost when the Axis forces surrendered in Tunisia in May 1943. The first would be resurrected as the 15th Panzergrenadier Division in Sicily, and the 21st Panzer Division was reformed in Normandy. The 10th Panzer Division shipped to Tunisia in late 1942 was also lost and was never reformed. At the time of the surrender, the Afrika Korps still had almost seventy panzers but no petrol. Rommel wanted to be with them at the end, but Hitler did not want another field marshal being captured and refused to allow him to return to Tunisia. Instead it was a very depressed General von Arnim who went into captivity with almost a quarter of a million men.

This is how Nazi propaganda portrayed the Afrika Korps to the German public on a picture postcard, part of a set on the armed forces. It presented a heroic image with the panzers roaring into action amid the palm trees. Fortunately, the work of the PK-reporters was not as crude as this.

North Africa Chronology: Key Events

1940

10 June: Benito Mussolini declares war on Britain and France.

13 September: Mussolini belatedly invades Egypt from Italian-controlled Libya and takes Sollum.

18 September: The Italians capture Sidi Barrani and dig in.

9 December: The British counterattack in the Western Desert with Operation *Compass* and the Italians fall back.

10 December: The Italians are driven from Sidi Barrani.

17 December: The British liberate Sollum and prepare to move into the eastern Libyan province of Cyrenaica.

1941

5 January: Australian forces take Bardia and 40,000 Italian prisoners.

22 January: British and Commonwealth forces capture the port of Tobruk.

3 February: Hitler orders the Luftwaffe to attack the British in Cyrenaica and orders two divisions be sent to Libya.

5 February: The British block the road at Beda Fomm. Hitler urges Mussolini to create a stop-line at Sirte.

6 February: Australian troops take Benghazi.

7 February: The Italian Army is cut off at Beda Fomm. Mussolini loses 130,000 men during the two-month-long British offensive.

12 February: General Erwin Rommel flies to Tripoli to prepare for the arrival of his Deutsches Afrika Korps with Operation *Sunflower*.

14 February: Reconnaissance and anti-tank units of the 5th Light Division arrive in Tripoli.

20 February: Rommel's troops make first contact with the British around El Aghelia.

11 March: The 5th Panzer Regiment belonging to the 5th Light Division disembarks at Tripoli.

31 March: Rommel launches his offensive to drive the British from Cyrenaica.

3 April: During the night German troops move into Benghazi.

6 April: The Germans take Mechili and the following day Derna.

10 April: The Afrika Korps reaches Tobruk but is unable to take it.

19 April: Rommel is almost killed when two British fighters strafe his command vehicle, just missing his head.

27 April: Rommel's troops occupy Halfaya Pass and the British retreat into Egypt.

15 May: The British conduct Operation *Brevity* to retake Halfaya Pass and fail.

15 June: The British attempt to relieve Tobruk with Operation *Battleaxe* and fail.

18 November: The British launch Operation *Crusader* to relieve Tobruk and drive Rommel from Cyrenaica.

19–22 November: Rommel gains a slight advantage in the tank battle for Sidi Rezegh.

28 November: Field Marshal Albert Kesselring arrives in Rome to take up the role of German C-in-C South.

8 December: Rommel, after failing to stop *Crusader*, withdraws rather than let the Afrika Korps be destroyed.

10 December: The British relieve Tobruk and Rommel retreats to Gazala and then El Aghelia.

24 December: The British take Benghazi.

28–30 December: Rommel halts the British advance.

1942

21 January: Rommel strikes back and the Afrika Korps moves forward swiftly.

29 January: The Germans take Benghazi.

7 February: Rommel is halted on the Gazala line held by the British 8th Army.

26 May: Rommel attacks the Gazala line and turns the British flank.

30 May: German armour is withdrawn into the 'Cauldron' which is protected by an anti-tank gun screen.

5 June: The British attack the 'Cauldron' and are repulsed. Rommel counterattacks.

13 June: The British start withdrawing from Gazala.

21 June: Rommel pierces the defences of Tobruk and captures almost 33,000 British and South African troops. He is promoted to field marshal.

28 June: Rommel takes Mersa Matruh in Egypt.

1 July: The British make a stand at El Alamein, resulting in the first battle of Alamein.

22 July: Both sides fight to a standstill.

13 August: General Montgomery takes command of the British 8th Army.

30 August: Rommel again attempts to fight his way through the British defences but is stopped at Alam Halfa.

6 September: Rommel withdraws to his start line.

23 October: Montgomery starts Operation *Lightfoot*, heralding the second battle of Alamein. His armour is unable to break through.

27 October: Rommel counterattacks but is held.

1 November: Montgomery launches Operation *Supercharger* and overwhelms Rommel.

4 November: Montgomery breaks through the Axis defences, but Rommel is already withdrawing towards Libya.

8 November: Anglo-American landings in Algeria and Morocco mean Rommel is trapped.

9 November: Hitler sends troops to occupy Tunisia.

13 November: Montgomery retakes Tobruk.

15 November. Montgomery recaptures Benghazi.

28 November: Rommel unsuccessfully urges Hitler to evacuate North Africa.

13 December: Rommel retreats from El Aghelia.

25 December: Montgomery takes Sirte.

1943

22 January: Rommel evacuates Tripoli and the following day the 8th Army arrives.

4 February: Montgomery advances into Tunisia.

14 February: Rommel and von Arnim successfully halt the Americans at the Kasserine Pass in western Tunisia.

6 March: Rommel counterattacks the British at Medenine in southern Tunisia and is repulsed with heavy losses.

10 March: Rommel visits Hitler and is not permitted to return to Tunisia. General von Arnim takes command of Army Group Afrika.

27 March: New Zealand troops force the Tebaga Gap, obliging the Afrika Korps to evacuate the Mareth Line.

28 April: The remains of the Afrika Korps launch a counterattack against the British at Jebel Bou Aoukaz.

7 May: Allies take Tunis and Bizerta.

12 May: Von Arnim surrenders and 240,000 Axis troops are captured, ending the war in North Africa.

Part One

The Deutsches Afrika Korps Arrives

1 Preparations

GENERAL VON THOMA FLEW TO Libya in October 1940 to assess whether German troops should be sent to help the Italians drive the British from Egypt. He liaised with the Italian commander Marshal Rodolfo Graziani and then made his report. Von Thoma astutely noted that resupply would be a major problem, especially as the Royal Navy dominated the Mediterranean. His report concluded, 'it would not be possible to maintain a large German Army there as well as the Italian Army.' Von Thoma cautioned that if troops were sent they should be armoured and consist of four panzer divisions. This force could only be maintained in an advance on the Nile if the Italian troops were replaced by Germans. The Italian generals were completely against the latter and indeed at the time did not want German help.

While Mussolini wanted Hitler's assistance, he also wanted all the glory of taking Egypt. Ironically, had Mussolini and Hitler acted sooner, they could have prevented the Italian defeat at Beda Fomm. However, in light of the large size of the Italian Army, Hitler felt it did not need his help and was only prepared to send a single panzer division as a token of solidarity. General Hans von Funck visited Tripoli on 26 January 1941 and concluded that a single division would be insufficient in light of the idea being swiftly resurrected by Hitler. On 1 February 1941 the German High Command agreed that with the British in Bardia and Tobruk there was little point sending troops to save a lost cause. Hitler took no notice and two days later ordered the movement of the 5th Light Division to Libya, to be followed by a second division.

Above: Once Hitler decided to commit to helping Mussolini keep his Libyan empire, Luftwaffe liaison officers were sent to Italy and Sicily to pave the way for the deployment of the Afrika Korps. The two officers on either end are wearing the standard Luftwaffe tropical dress, which on the whole was more comfortable and practical than that issued to the Army. Neither of them is wearing a jacket and they must have been much cooler than their colleagues in the full blue-grey uniform.

Opposite: Three men off to war photographed in Altötting, Bavaria, in early 1941. The Gefreiter or lance corporal on the left is headed for the desert. He is presumably saying goodbye to family members, possibly his father and brother, who are officers in the Army and Luftwaffe respectively. The prospect of deploying to North Africa must have seemed highly exciting for this young man until reality cut in. He is dressed in tropical field service jacket with the national eagle on his right breast in blue grey with tan background. Under the jacket is the tropical shirt – he would soon discard the tie. His *Bergmütze* or peaked field cap would be a valued piece of kit.

Luftwaffe officers belonging to Luftlotte 2, or 2nd Air Fleet, enjoying a glass of wine and a smoke in Sicily. The Germans made use of the Italians' Sicilian air bases to supply their troops in Libya and attack Malta. Both are in shirtsleeve order.

This Luftwaffe pilot, Major Bindewald with Luftflotte 2, also photographed in Sicily, has an almost pink tropical jacket that contrasts sharply with his sand-coloured trousers. In the Luftwaffe the rank of major was equivalent to a British squadron leader.

What appear to be two army sergeant majors and a sergeant prepare for deployment. They are also wearing the peaked field cap; German forces sent to Libya were equipped with a variety of headgear, not all of it was as useful as intended.

Above: The 5th Light Division, an ad hoc unit formed using elements of the 3rd Panzer Division, was the first to ship to Tripoli. The division was deployed in such haste that there was no time to paint over its vehicles' European *dunkel grau* (dark grey). This meant that cars such as this Horch 830 had to wait until they were in Libya before being overpainted in *gelb braun* (yellow brown) or *dunkel gelb* (dark yellow). The Horch 830 was built in a number of guises that included a signals car and a signals van.

Left: Members of a German flak unit, identifiable by the red *Waffenfarben* (corps colours) on their collars, fraternising with Italian civilians. They still retain their standard-issue Luftwaffe uniforms. Troops and equipment arrived in Italy by train and were then shipped to Sicily and on to Libya. Naples became a major hub for German operations.

Part of the 75th Artillery Regiment seen here in Leipzig, also from 3rd Panzer, was sent to give the 5th Light Division fire support. Prime movers such as this Sd Kfz (Sonderkraftahrzeug – special-purpose motor vehicle) 6 and its larger cousins the Sd Kfz 7 and 8 were used to tow artillery in North Africa. The semi-tracks or half-tracks generally coped much better with the desert conditions than the all-wheeled vehicles.

WH-52716
WH-52716

These 150mm guns are towed by the 12-ton Sd Kfz 8 half-track. A panzer artillery regiment was supposed to have twenty-four 105mm howitzers and eight 150mm howitzers, but the 5th Light Division had nothing like these numbers when it first landed in Tripoli. During February 1941 it could muster just three batteries of guns, supported by calibration and signals detachments.

WH-177971
WH-177971

Above: One of the most important weapons that Rommel took with him was the towed 88mm flak gun. Designed as an anti-aircraft weapon, it could also be used in an anti-tank role. Rommel often denuded his air defences so the '88' could support the panzers at the front. This example was photographed in Halle, Germany.

Opposite: German liaison officers sightseeing in Italy or Sicily. Note that their militarised civilian sedan remains in panzer grey.

Achtung!
Doppelschrauben

Freighters such as this were used to ferry the Afrika Korps and Italian divisions to Tripoli. The Italian Navy was also employed to ship troops and supplies across to Libya. Although Italy lacked aircraft carriers, the Regia Aeronautica was able to provide air cover from its numerous bases in Sicily.

Sailing from Naples was a big adventure but there was always the danger of attack by the Royal Navy and the RAF. These men watch nervously for their fighter escort provided either by the Luftwaffe or Regia Aeronautica.

Opposite inset: While at sea this Luftwaffe flak unit takes time to check their equipment and carry out essential maintenance. For air defence the 5th Light Division took with it five anti-aircraft batteries of the 33rd Flak Regiment, as well as three companies from the 606th Self-propelled Flak Battalion.

Anti-aircraft gunners put their 20mm flak gun through its paces. Such units were equipped with the Flak 30 and the Flakvierling 38, both of which were 20mm calibre guns. The 606th Battalion was equipped with the Sd Kfz 10/4, which consisted of a Demag D7 half-track armed with a 20mm flak gun.

Above: German soldiers and Luftwaffe flak personnel enjoy the sunshine. Rommel did not entirely trust the Italian air defences around Tripoli and understandably was keen to get his forces ashore and forward as quickly as possible.

Opposite: Despite wearing a life vest, this soldier does not look very confident. Once the Libyan coast came into view the men of the 5th Light Division were able to relax. One of the Axis's greatest fears was an attack by British submarines, as they went unseen.

2 Build-up in Tripoli

DESPITE GENERAL VON THOMA'S recommendation that Germany deploy four panzer divisions to North Africa, Hitler only agreed to send two. These were sent south by train via Austria to Naples ready to be shipped across to Tripoli. Some 40,000 troops would form the Afrika Korps, which was to support the 150,000 Italian soldiers still available in Libya after Beda Fomm. The first of these forces began to arrive in mid-February 1941. Mussolini also moved to reinforce Libya with additional Italian divisions.

Left: A German naval gunner stands watch by a flak gun protecting a freighter. He is wearing the standard navy-blue reefer jacket, or pea-coat, and matching trousers. His headgear is the side or boarding cap. German soldiers can be seen behind him unloading trucks. Clear skies always enticed air attack.

Opposite: This truck arrived in its *dunkel grau*, also known as panzer grey. This dark colour would make it stand out in the desert, so it needed to be repainted as soon as possible. Nonetheless, Rommel rushed much of his equipment to the front still in panzer grey. Portside 5th Light Division was supported by the 683rd Loading and 681st Unloading Special Employment Battalions.

Above: Having established their billets, the first thing many soldiers did was head for the nearest beach. These beachcombing Germans seem oblivious to the derelict freighter in front of them. The shiny back wheel on their Horch indicates that they have backed it into the sea. The man in the longer shorts is still wearing his standard European-issue black leather jackboots.

Opposite: A signalman with the 5th Light Division stands stiffly by his Auto Union Horch 901 car in Tripoli, February 1941. Again it is very conspicuous in panzer grey. The Horch 901 entered service in 1937 as a universal medium cross-country car. It saw extensive action in North Africa. The man's tropical uniform looks brand new. By the summer the 200th Signals Battalion consisted of two companies supported by a signals supply column.

Like so many vehicles, this Horch was sent to the front still panzer grey. However, much of the car is plastered in dust and sand which has helped to break up its outline. The bonnet or hood remains pristine but the crew have placed camouflage netting over it.

Trucks in more appropriate desert colours, though all three are different. These are German-built Ford G398TS. A number of Ford designs were produced before and during the war in Cologne for the German armed forces. A half-track variant was built for use on the Eastern Front. The Afrika Korps also deployed various versions of the Opel Blitz and the Phänomen Granit.

More trucks being off-loaded but ill-suited for their desert role. The vessels and their cargo were always at risk of air attack and it was best to get everything off as quickly as possible. Rommel's adjutant Lieutenant Colonel Hans-Joachim Schraepler complained, 'We always lack loading capacity. A large quantity of supplies has arrived in Tripoli, but we could not transport it.'

Opposite inset: The last lorry looks precariously balanced on the crane. From the cab it seems to be some sort of Fiat. Mussolini also rushed reinforcements, including the Ariete Armoured Division, to Libya to replace his forces lost at Beda Fomm.

Above: A ferry transporting at least half a dozen German Ford trucks heads for the quay. These vehicles are sporting a desert camouflage.

Below: Italian-built trucks queuing to take on supplies. The Afrika Korps was regularly short of transport and was swift to requisition abandoned Italian equipment. Reconditioned Italian cars, motorcycles and lorries were placed under new ownership and adorned with the palm tree and swastika insignia of the Afrika Korps. When the Italians complained, Rommel ignored them.

Above: Supply trucks head off into town to find their assigned units' depots. The lorry in the distance is loaded with crates.

Opposite: An honour guard presents arms as the Nazi swastika is hoisted over North Africa. It is interesting to note that the colours of their uniforms do not match. They are wearing three pieces of kit that were largely replaced in the Libyan and Egyptian deserts.

Above: The calf-length desert boot, which consisted of a brown hard leather shoe attached to a tan soft canvas lace-up upper part, seemed a good idea. It was intended to protect the lower leg and keep out the sand and biting insects. However, it was time consuming to put on and take off. This was a particular problem if a soldier was wounded in the leg or foot, which meant all the laces had to be cut. Prolonged wear could also cause skin irritation. Many men later opted for the soft ankle boot that was made in the same style. However, the long desert variant continued in use throughout the fighting in North Africa, including the Tunisian campaign.

Opposite: The sun helmet or *Tropische Kopfbedeckung* was not a success either. It came in three styles: one with greenish drill fabric over cork, one of brown felt and a non-standard wicker version. The helmet insignia were in the form of pin-back metal shields. On the left was the German eagle badge, while on the right was the black/white/red shield. The jodhpurs or riding breeches were replaced by baggy trousers or shorts, though they remained popular with officers.

Above: One of the Afrika Korps' first tasks was to establish all the necessary ancillary services. German doctors and medics set up shop. They are much more casually attired. The relaxed German attitude to uniforms in the desert never reached the same proportions as those of British troops serving with the 8th Army. The 5th Light Division's support troops included a field hospital with two medical companies and two ambulance companies.

Opposite above: The same medical team pose proudly with their ambulance. The Phänomen Granit 1500 was built by the Phänomen-Werke Gustav Hiller in Zittau with either cargo or box van bodywork. The latter were mainly employed as ambulances. The Kfz 70 was a utility car variant fitted with desert tyres.

Opposite below: Enjoying the sunshine on the roof of their new billet. The soldier on the left appears to be wearing the German Wound Badge in Silver, Second Class, on his left breast pocket. The badge was awarded if the recipient had been wounded three or four times.

WH
510149

Above: Desert acclimatisation. Signals troops adapt to life in the desert outside Tripoli. The vehicles are still awaiting repainting.

Below: A forward German repair workshop out in the open desert ready to assist in the coming campaign. The Germans excelled in the battlefield recovery of damaged equipment, especially armour, which regularly helped lessen their combat losses.

The field postal service, along with catering, entertainment and pay, was also needed to sustain the Afrika Korps. This soldier is with a signals unit outside Tripoli in February 1941. The box would have been the property of the 735th Motorised Field Post Office.

3 Meet the Locals

LIBYA WAS FAR FROM a dusty backwater. The Italians had done all they could to modernise the coastal cities and improve communications between them and metropolitan Italy. The Via Balbia, the coastal road opened by Mussolini in 1937, ran through Tripoli west to the Tunisian border and east to the Egyptian border. 'I came to know Tripolitania very well from the air,' wrote Rommel, 'and formed a great admiration for the colonising achievements of the Italians. They had left their mark all over the country, particularly round Tripoli, Tarhuna and Homs.' However, he was disappointed that the Italians had not built a railway along the coast.

Italian forces in the country in early 1941 consisted of a mix of metropolitan army divisions, so-called elite Blackshirt divisions drawn from the Fascist militia and Libyan colonial divisions. Rommel never really trusted the Italian military and kept his plans secret until the very last moment, which made for a very troubled relationship. While the Italian military and Italian colonists welcomed the Afrika Korps, the Libyans were not so enthusiastic.

This is what greeted the Germans so far from home. By 1941 Tripoli was a modern cosmopolitan city with tree-lined boulevards, new civic buildings and luxury hotels. Before the war it became a playground for the wealthy and hosted the annual Tripoli Grand Prix. It annoyed the Italians immensely that German-built Mercedes-Benz racing cars kept beating their Alfa Romeos.

Above: Benghazi had also been turned into a playground for Italians. The Lungomare or sea walk was a place for promenading; note the Romulus and Remus statue on the left. This was all part of Mussolini's ill-fated endeavour to recreate the Roman Empire. After Benghazi was captured by the Australians on 6 February 1941, British and Commonwealth troops posed a threat to Tripoli and the western province of Tripolitania.

Below: When Rommel retook Benghazi on 3 April 1941 his PK-reporters or Kriegsberichter were able to photograph the neoclassical Benghazi Roman Catholic Cathedral at their leisure. This building had taken a decade to build and had only just been finished at the outbreak of war. Benghazi, which continued to change hands regularly, became an operating base for the Afrika Korps and hosted a popular German cinema for troops on leave.

Km 34
A.BREVIGLIERI
HUNA

Above: A patrol rides out led by an Italian officer wearing the Italian-style tropical field cap. He is also attired in the officer's double-breasted greatcoat; his single cuff stripe indicates he is a second lieutenant. The Germans were intrigued by the Italian Army's colonial units. The Royal Corps of Libyan Troops comprised cavalry and infantry. The former was organised into squadron groups, consisting of a headquarters and four squadrons each of 150 men. The Italians also had camel-mounted and motorised Saharan troops.

Opposite inset: A German liaison officer getting to know the locals. The Libyans, who had been brutalised by the Italians for three decades, had little reason to welcome the presence of the Afrika Korps as it would simply prop up Mussolini's colonial regime.

Opposite: Italian soldiers and Libyan civilians photographed in Tarhuna, south-east of Tripoli. The soldiers are kitted out with the Italian khaki drill tropical uniform and side cap known as the *bustina*. Mussolini began reinforcing his troops in the provinces of Tripolitania and Cyrenaica in early 1941 with the arrival of the Ariete Armoured Division. This, along with the Trieste Motorised Division, formed the 20th Army Manoeuvre Corps under General Gastone Gambara. The battered 21st Corps under General Enea Navarrini was rebuilt using five metropolitan infantry divisions. Mussolini ended up sending three armoured and two motorised divisions to Libya.

The camel-mounted Sahariana consisted of only two companies totalling about 600 men. They were intended for policing duties in the interior rather than fighting the British.

This Sahariana is armed with the Italian Carcano cavalry carbine. His headgear is a red tarbush or fez. The Compagnia Sahariana or motorised Saharan troops tended to be much better equipped, with motor transport, heavy machine guns and anti-tank guns.

Above: Mussolini had two regular Libyan infantry divisions at the start of the Second World War. These troops wore a combination of Italian uniform and local dress. Each battalion was identified by a different colour tarbush and sash. This guardsman has standard Italian webbing, pouches and the standard single-breasted Italian Army greatcoat. He is armed with the Italian Mannlicher-Carano rifle. By the time the Afrika Korps arrived, the 1st and 2nd Libyan Divisions had been lost and the survivors were relegated to security duties. Neither unit was reformed.

Opposite: Libyan orderlies had to meet their Italian officers' every need. While the officers lived in the lap of luxury, their soldiers often existed in abject squalor, especially those in the desolate frontier forts. The Germans and the British disapproved of the vast gulf that existed between Italian officers and their men. Rommel made it a point to share the hardships of his troops. Smartly turned out, the orderly is from the same unit as the previous Sahariana – he has matching colour tarbush and sash.

Above: Members of an Arab caravan smile at the German photographer. The man on the left intriguingly seems to be wearing some sort of military-style canvas boot. They do not appear to be carrying weapons.

Opposite: This former Libyan soldier now makes a living selling bread. He is old enough to remember the invasion of 1911 when Italy seized control of Libya from the Ottoman Empire. Mussolini crushed Libyan resistance during the 1920s by forcing 100,000 people out of the Jebel Akhdar and into concentration camps, where many of them died. Prominent resistance leader Omar al-Mukhtar was executed in 1931.

The caravan takes a break. On the whole the indigenous people of North Africa tried to avoid the fighting between the European powers. Libyan colonial forces understandably had little desire to die for their Italian masters or indeed the Germans.

The weather-beaten face of rural North Africa. The Arabs and Berbers endured wars of colonial conquest by the British, French, Italians and Spanish. The war started by Mussolini in 1940 with his invasion of Egypt was to be on a much vaster scale than all the previous conflicts.

Inevitably the cities, towns and villages of northern Libya were to change hands on numerous occasions and suffered extensive damage as a result.

A German soldier tries out his Arabic with a Libyan soldier. The latter is wearing the Italian double-breasted greatcoat which was also issued to warrant officers and sergeants.

German medics fooling around in Italian uniform. The man on the right is wearing a rather small Italian officer's jacket. The Italians also wore a much larger bush or safari jacket known as the *Sahariana*. This was so comfortable that German officers and even British officers were known to wear it in the field. The medics' ambulance is parked just behind them on the right.

Above: While the Germans were entranced by the beauty of North Africa, they were less enraptured by the Italian administration and military.

Below: Garrison life outside the major towns and cities along the Via Balbia was less pleasant. Note the freshly dug twin gun emplacement in the middle ground.

Part Two

Hardware of War

4 Panzer Group Afrika

THE 5TH PANZER REGIMENT arrived in Tripoli with 150 panzers. These comprised seventy light Mk IIs, while the rest were Mk IIIs armed with the L/42 50mm gun or Mk IVs with the L/24 75mm gun. The 5th and 8th Panzer Regiments took just forty Mk IV Ausf. D and E models. The Mk III was by far the most common panzer and there were often two to one for every Mk II and IV. By March 1941 the Afrika Korps had gathered nearly 160 panzers, supported by sixty Italian tanks. The Italians were very pleased to see Rommel's panzers. They had lost 500 tanks, including the Babini Armoured Brigade and thousands of wheeled vehicles to the British advance in Cyrenaica.

One of the first units to come ashore was the 5th Light Division's 3rd Reconnaissance Battalion. Such units were equipped with the little four-wheeled Sd Kfz 222 and the larger eight-wheeled Sd Kfz 231 seen here and 234 armoured cars. The latter types had the best cross-country performance and on occasions armoured cars were more mobile than tanks. However, they sometimes struggled on slopes and in soft sand. Rommel's first action was to send the battalion up to Sirte to bolster the Italian defences.

Above: The outline of this Panzer IV is obscured by all the extra kit covering it, which includes a large storage crate, camouflage netting and jerrycans. The horizontal rusty cylindrical object is the distinctive engine silencer and exhaust outlet fitted to the Mk IVs. This was replaced on the final Ausf. J by two simple vertical exhaust mufflers. The rear left track guard has been snagged on something and bent out of shape. As the crew are wearing greatcoats it is obviously not that warm.

Opposite above: German Panzertruppen gather around an early model Panzer III armed with the short 50mm KwK L/42 tank gun, which equipped the Ausf. G and H models. Subsequent versions had the more powerful long 50mm KwK39 L/60 gun. Judging from the front drive sprocket and rear idler, this example with probably an Ausf. G.

Opposite below: The tank roars off into the desert, throwing up a great cloud of dust. To cope with these conditions, the engine and oil-cleaner cooling fan on the Ausf. G (Tropical) were modified with extra air filters fitted. The heat was to be a problem for the Panzertruppen and their panzers, though. Rommel recorded on 2 June 1941, 'Tanks standing in the sun go up to as much as 160°, which is too hot to touch.'

A fine shot of a Panzer III and its commander at sunset. Some 600 Ausf. Gs were built between April 1940 and February 1941, while 308 Ausf. Hs were produced from October 1940 to April 1941; many of them ended up in North Africa.

Above: The photographer has stopped to record this approaching convoy led by a half-track. To the rear is another one towing a flatbed trailer carrying a small armoured fighting vehicle. This unit belonged to the 605th Panzerjäger Battalion, which formed part of the 5th Light Division.

Right: The vehicle on the trailer is clearly of interest to the photographer to the right of the frame. It is a Panzerjäger I consisting of the Panzer I Ausf. B chassis armed with a Czech 47mm gun in a limited traverse mounting. The Panzerjäger Is of the 605th Panzerjäger Battalion were shipped to Tripoli still in their panzer grey. The crews soon painted them and fitted the three-sided gun shield with a canvas cover over the rear and the top of the fighting compartment, which was otherwise open to the elements.

Opposite above: Panzertruppen on parade south of Tunis in 1943. Behind the group of officers on the right is an olive-green Panzer III. This colour was more favourable for the Tunisian landscape than sand colour. These men probably belong to the 7th Panzer Regiment, 10th Panzer Division, which was shipped to Tunisia in December 1942.

Opposite below: The short barrel on this Panzer III indicates it is either an Ausf. H or an early Ausf. J. The side-on view gives a good impression on how the colour scheme helped the tank blend in with the local terrain. Many of the Ausf. Js, which were built between March 1941 and June 1942, were sent to North Africa as combat replacements.

Right: Another view of the lead vehicle. Rommel received sixty-six of the initial series Marder III. They first arrived in North Africa in May 1942 and supported Panzer Army Afrika headquarters. Subsequent deliveries from July to November 1942 were assigned to the 33rd Panzerjäger Battalion with the 15th Panzer Division and the 39th Panzerjäger Battalion.

Below: This row of seven Marder IIIs are in the port of La Goulette, Tunisia, in 1942. The first is a Panzerjäger 38(t) für 76.2mm PaK36(r) (Sd Kfz 139) comprising the chassis of the Czech-built Panzer 38(t) and a captured Soviet gun. The first vehicle has a trailer which may have been for extra ammunition. The others are the slightly later 75mm PaK40/3 Panzer 38(t) Ausf. H (Sd Kfz 138) that was armed with the German PaK40 anti-tank gun.

Although both versions of the Marder III were well armed, the high profile and open fighting compartment meant the crew were vulnerable to both direct and indirect fire.

These Marder IIIs look as if they have just been delivered. They all have water drums, plus crates of extra ammunition. Each has stowage for jerrycans and a canvas tent fitted over the fighting compartment.

Opposite: On 7–8 April 1941 during the fighting at Mechili, Rommel captured three British AEC Dorchester armoured command vehicles. These monsters were dubbed Mammut or Mammoth by the Germans. Rommel kept one, which was named Max; the second, called Moritz, was given to Major General Ludwig Crüwell and the third was issued to General Johannes Streich.

Below left: Lieutenant Heinz Werner Schmidt noted Rommel watching the contents of the Mammoths being emptied. 'Among the stuff turned out', recalled Schmidt, 'he spotted a pair of large sun-and-sand goggles. ... Those goggles for ever after were to be the insignia of the "Desert Fox".'

Below right: The only windows on these vehicles were for the driver and the passenger, which reduced them to very hot steel boxes. Nonetheless, Rommel used his to visit the front line. Schmidt adds, 'He had the German cross painted on them all.' Rommel's almost became his coffin when strafed by an enemy fighter on 19 April 1941. The rounds came through the open windows, wounding the driver and narrowly missing the General.

5 Beware the '88'

ROMMEL PIONEERED THE USE of anti-tank guns as offensive and defensive weapons. The most notable weapon he had in North Africa was the towed 88mm flak gun. He discovered during an emergency trying to fend off British Matilda tanks at Arras in France in 1940 that the '88' was also an effective tank killer. This had led to anti-tank and tank gun variants of the '88', but in North Africa Rommel continued to employ the flak version in a dual role. His main anti-tank gun was the towed 50mm L/42 and later the L/60 PaK38. The much more capable 75mm PaK40 only saw limited action towards the end of the fighting in North Africa. As German tank guns fired both armour-piercing rounds and high explosives, the German Army made less use of conventional towed artillery in North Africa than in other theatres of operation. However, field artillery did include 105mm, 150mm and 210mm guns.

An Italian officer peers through a scissor telescope while a German soldier looks on. This is the Zeiss Scherenfernrohr, a cross between binoculars and a periscope, which was designed to enable the user to remain concealed. A field artillery model was produced for laying field guns and measuring shell burst heights.

The Italian soldier in the foreground looks rather pensive. Perhaps their fire has fallen short. The Italians had large quantities of 75mm and 100mm guns in Cyrenaica, but they lost 1,000 guns to the British, including 400 at Bardia and 200 at Tobruk. The standard Italian field gun was the deficient 75/27 75mm gun. This only had a range of 9,000 metres and even then it needed additional elevation, using a pit for the trail.

Above: This German flak gunner indulges in a bit of sunbathing while on duty. The Afrika Korps took a variety of 20mm, 37mm and 88mm anti-aircraft guns to North Africa. The best Italian anti-aircraft gun was the Ansaldo 75/46, which like the German '88' could also be used in an anti-tank role.

Below: The German 88mm Flak 18/36/37 gun was Rommel's most prized tank destroyer, which outranged all British tank guns. In June 1941 during Operation *Battleaxe* it was reckoned that every '88' round fired claimed a British tank. For transport the gun was fitted with a two-wheel limber at the front and back. Although an excellent tank killer, its high exposed carriage made it and the crew vulnerable to British shelling and bombing. The Italians developed a 90mm anti-aircraft gun but it did not enter service until 1943.

As Rommel anticipated, the arrival of the '88' in North Africa swiftly ended the British Matilda II tank's dominance of the battlefield. It had reigned supreme over the Italians, who had no answer to its thick armour. These British prisoners of war were taken during Rommel's re-conquest of Cyrenaica. Behind them is an abandoned Matilda II and off to its left and right are British Valentine tanks.

Above: More PoWs. Behind them are two knocked-out Valentine tanks. The Valentine suffered the same fate as the Matilda at the hands of Rommel's guns and panzers; however, unlike the Matilda, it was not withdrawn from service in North Africa.

Below: The German 37mm PaK35/36 was the standard German anti-tank gun in 1939. It and the larger 50mm PaK38 were both deployed to North Africa with the Afrika Korps. The crew are stocking up on fuel, judging by the pile of jerrycans.

Above: A German observation post high among the rocks. High ground became tactically vital because whoever held it could survey the battlefield for miles around. For the siege of Tobruk Rommel created the 104th Artillery Command, which included thirty-six Italian 105mm guns, eighty-four Italian 149mm guns, twelve French 100mm guns and forty French 150mm guns.

Above : This German gunner is firing the 150mm sFH 18 heavy field howitzer. A battery normally consisted of four guns that were towed by half-tracks. The German 210mm Mrs 18 heavy field gun was very accurate but its weight meant it was not very manoeuvrable. At the end of June 1942 Rommel recorded, 'Great booty had fallen to the Afrika Korps, including a British 150-mm. battery, which they had immediately put back into action again.'

Above : A German column, which includes captured British Quad artillery tractors, taking a break at Siwa. The palm trees contrast starkly with the open desert.

Main picture: The results of German shelling or air attack on a British transport column. The towed weapon in the centre is the 40mm Bofors L/60 anti-aircraft gun. The scattered debris is the result of looting by the Afrika Korps. By the summer of 1941 the 21st Panzer Division included the 155th Artillery Regiment with nine batteries of 105mm and 150mm guns.

6 Don't Spare the Suspension

THE GERMANS EMPLOYED A wide variety of wheeled and half-track vehicles in North Africa. General transport and towing vehicles included the Volkswagen Kübelwagen utility car and the Opel Blitz and Phänomen Granit trucks, while half-tracks included the Sd Kfz 7, 8, 10, 11, 250 and 251. The Germans also used large numbers of captured British and French lorries and were known to requisition Italian ones. The half-tracks were less prone to getting stuck than all-wheeled vehicles so Rommel used them on the front line to tow guns as well as transport ammunition and other supplies. Wheeled vehicles tended to carry out ambulance, transport and supply tasks in the rear areas.

Main photograph: The ubiquitous and hardy Kfz 1 Volkswagen Type 82, better known as the Kübelwagen, was the German equivalent of the famous American Willys Jeep. It went into production in March 1941 and Rommel realised it would be ideal for deployment in the desert. This vehicle is being used by a PK-reporter somewhere outside Tarhuna and is clearly brown in colour. It is fitted with standard European tyres, but the spare is a much larger sand tyre.

Opposite inset: The cameraman has hopped out of the Kübelwagen and photographed the rolling semi-arid farmland. The windscreen is cracked, the damage probably caused by debris flying off the terrible roads.

Above: The crew of a camouflaged Kübelwagen and a sedan stop to enjoy a gelato from a nearby Italian store somewhere in Sicily. The man on the left looks rather incongruous in his black leather jackboots. The neighbouring *alimentari* or food store would be a welcome opportunity to stock up on fresh fruit and vegetables.

Opposite: The reporter and his driver roll into an oasis. By the end of the war over 52,000 Kübelwagens had been built. Its light weight of just half a ton meant a two-man crew could manhandle it out of soft sand and mud.

Above: The Opel Blitz 4x2 light cargo and 4x4 medium trucks were another common sight in North Africa. The WL on the number plate means this vehicle belongs to a Luftwaffe unit. The driver and his mechanic have tried to shade the tyres from the heat of the midday sun. This may also have been done to reduce the amount of dust thrown up by the wheels, though the canvas would likely have snagged in the wheel arches.

Opposite: The driver appears to be wearing a captured South African Army sun helmet. This was smaller than the unpopular German variant. Stocks were seized and for a while they were widely used by German troops. His Opel Blitz looks almost factory fresh.

Above: The same column tries to make friends with the locals. One of the problems faced by Luftwaffe ground crews was that while the aircrews could swiftly land on liberated airfields and makeshift air strips, they had to play catch-up. Again note how the wheels have been covered.

Below: Time for some maintenance. The driver of this German-built Ford is checking his engine beneath the welcome shade of a large palm tree. If vehicles were not maintained properly overheating became a problem.

Above: What appears to be an Opel Blitz Kfz 305 signals van has become a leaning post for its crew. Opels were built by Adam Opel AG at their Brandenburg/Havel plant throughout the war. The 305 series were known as Koffer-Aufbau or box vans. The objects stacked on the roof of the cab are jerrycans.

Below: A bogged-down Opel gets a welcome tow from a Demag D7 or Sd Kfz half-track. The surrounding ground has already been churned up by other tracked vehicles.

Above: Another Luftwaffe convoy who have stopped for a break. On the left is a Renault AHS cargo truck. This vehicle was built specifically for the Wehrmacht during the German occupation of France as the LKW 2t Renault(f). The Renault AHN and AHR and the Matford F917WS were also produced for use by the German military.

Below: Lieutenant Colonel Hans Cramer, commander of the 15th Panzer Division's 8th Panzer Regiment, visiting his men using a Horch 901. In February 1943 he took charge of the Afrika Korps.

Right: The crew of this Horch 901 belonging to the 200th Signals Battalion, 5th Light Division, were so pleased with their camouflage efforts that they stopped at the roadside to photograph it.

Right: They were then less happy after they got it bogged down in wet sand following a rain storm. On this occasion the V-8 engine has done nothing but dig it in deeper. The chassis for this type of vehicle were produced until 1943 by both the Horch and Wanderer divisions of Auto Union.

Below: In contrast, this vehicle is concealed amid scrubland and very dry sand.

These two shots (inset above and opposite) show a Horch belonging to the 21st Panzer Division partially sheltered from the sun by an awning. The divided D divisional logo can just be seen on the lower right. The 5th Light Division was redesignated 21st Panzer on 1 August 1941.

A column of very rusty-looking Italian lorries requisitioned by the Afrika Korps winds its way up the coast road. German mechanics quickly got abandoned Italian vehicles running and appropriated them into service.

Above: The Germans also made use of captured British equipment such as this Morris C8 artillery tractor. Known as the Quad, it was used to tow the British 25-pounder field gun. To avoid friendly fire its new owners have painted the *Balkenkreuz* or German cross on the side.

Below: A British jeep is put to good use in German service. The driver is posing for the cameraman with his binoculars raised. The tracks in the sand always risked alerting enemy reconnaisance aircraft.

Above: Grinning joy riders with a captured British cab-less Morris CS8. The Germans regularly captured vast quantities of British equipment. At Tobruk they seized thousands of vehicles.

Below: This mechanic is doing some vital engine maintenance on the CS8 while topping up his tan. Supporting the 5th Light Division were the 122nd and 129th Motor Vehicle Repair Companies. These became the 2nd and 3rd Companies of the 200th Motor Repair Unit with the 21st Panzer.

Horribly exposed in the open, this unit has done it upmost to minimise the effects of an air attack. At least ten vehicles, comprising eight trucks and two staff cars, are visible and they are well spread out. Canvas awnings not only provided welcome shade but also helped to break up the shape of the vehicle from the air.

Axis transport vehicles were often in such short supply that British prisoners had to drive themselves into captivity. The PK-reporter who took this shot could not resist the propaganda opportunity.

Part Three

Out into the Desert

7 Baking at the Front

MEMBERS OF THE AFRIKA KORPS initially found North Africa a bit of a shock. The days were extremely hot and the nights were often cold. Rommel found night-time in the mountainous and forested Jebel Akhdar particularly chilly. In a rush to take the battle to the enemy, he gave his men very little time to acclimatise to desert life. By the summer they were boiling. 'A ferocious heat!' complained Rommel in late August 1941, 'so hot that one steams even in the early morning'.

This was the reality of war that faced the men of the Afrika Korps when they reached the front. A parched desert landscape with no cover for miles. Forward observation posts such as this were designed to keep an eye on enemy movements and warn of impending attack.

Above: The photographer stood up to take photographs of approaching British tanks. The normal response would be to call artillery fire or air attacks down on them, but Rommel soon became adept at luring British armour forward by withdrawing his panzers. British tanks would then run into a concealed 50mm and 88mm anti-tank gun screen as well as mines and the panzers would counterattack the survivors.

Below: Another forward position overlooking the same battlefield. The shallow scrape in which the man is leaning shows how difficult it was to dig in such terrain. He and his comrade have no cover from the sun and would be at risk of heat stroke if they stay there for too long.

Above: A colonel and his staff, concealed from enemy reconnaissance planes, take a midday meal in their forward headquarters. The olive-green canvas, camouflaged *Zeltbahn* and netting at least provide some shade from the sun. The seated officers are wearing the field cap, side cap and the tropical helmet.

Opposite: The colonel does not look entirely pleased with the field rations being doled out by his orderly. The grubby mess tins have seen a lot of action. They needed to eat quickly before the flies swarmed over everything.

Above: This shot shows how well the headquarters is concealed from a distance, and especially from the air it would become invisible among the scrub. The staff car at the top of the rise, though, is a bit of a giveaway. Furthermore, the diners appear to have an uninvited guest in the shape of a Libyan camel. Note what appears to be an inflatable air bed.

Opposite: The camel finally loses interest and wanders back towards the cameraman. The colonel's staff car has been left to bake in the sun.

Above: Judging from their pristine uniforms these men are newly arrived at the front. Their clothing is of a uniform colour and style. This would change once they started personalising their kit to make it as comfortable as possible.

Opposite above: A sergeant and some of his men have found an oasis and the shade of some palm trees to prepare a meal. Whatever they are cooking came out of the two tins to the right. The men are all wearing field caps, long-sleeved shirts and rolled-up shorts.

Opposite below: This soldier has shown some ingenuity by creating his own oven, complete with tin stove pipe. The jerrycan by his knee contains water.

This man also looks like a newbie. The tropical helmets were soon discarded as impractical. They were too large to be worn inside vehicles and the men opted for caps.

Above: A coastal camp such as this would be considered luxury. The rocks provided shelter and the men could swim and bathe in the sea. The local Libyans were highly amused and affronted by the German habit of stripping off at the first sign of water. The white buttocks of the man in the middle are glinting in the sunlight.

Below: Another view of the same billet. Life under canvas was baking hot during the day and chilly at night. The men also had to be careful that they were not sharing their beds with scorpions or other creepy-crawlies.

Above: Not all the local wildlife was hostile. This officer has found himself host to a chameleon, which was preferable to a scorpion. These creatures were handy to have about as they live off insects.

Above right: Unsure if it is about to become dinner for the Afrika Korps, the chameleon has hunched itself into a protective ball. When picked up they tend to turn a darker colour.

Right: Another soldier plays with a chameleon. These reptiles needed vegetation for their habitat so were found near watering holes and in scrubland.

Opposite: Often the Afrika Korps did not have the luxury of sleeping in a tent. As the war ebbed and flowed along the North African coast the troops regularly slept in their vehicles or on the ground around them.

Above: The honour guard turn eyes left as their former comrade is lowered into the ground. Although the men have been spared the formality of wearing their webbing, helmets were always considered appropriate headgear for German military funerals.

A more sombre occasion. German infantry escort a fallen comrade to the cemetery. Repatriating the dead home was simply not practical, so fatalities were buried locally in well-tended and presented cemeteries.

Above: Once the burial is complete, the honour guard lift their Mauser rifles and fire in salute. The officer to the left gives the Nazi salute.

This portrait shows war reporter Fritz Moosmüller contemplating the battles to come. He has a newly bestowed Iron Cross Second Class. Normally just the ribbon was displayed from the tunic button hole, the cross was usually only worn on the day of the award.

Above: This sand storm whipping across the Via Balbia is mild compared to some which reduced visibility to almost nothing. 'Sometimes the dust-clouds were so thick', said Rommel, 'you could only see two to three yards.'

Below: Temperatures were cooler in the mountains, where Rommel and his men frequently suffered from the cold during the night.

8 Rommel's Achilles Heel

THE CHINK IN ROMMEL'S armour was his very long lines of communication across the Mediterranean and along the North African coast. His commanders despaired at his lack of attention to the Afrika Korps' logistical requirements and the difficulties they faced. Moving supplies by air, sea and land proved to be a major problem. 'The loading and unloading organisation worked far too leisurely,' complained Field Marshal Kesselring, the German Commander-in-Chief South. 'The unloaded stuff was left about on the quays for an unconscionable length of time and in this was sometimes sacrificed to bombs.' Rommel recorded on 29 September 1941, 'A large shipment arrived for us at Benghazi. It took 50 hours to unload.'

Luftwaffe personnel watching the results of an air attack on Tripoli. The port was a vital supply point for sustaining Rommel's war effort. Ammunition, food, fuel, personnel and equipment all had to be shipped over from Italy. Petrol barges moored to the west of Tripoli were used to move fuel up the coast to the Afrika Korps. Smaller vessels were likewise employed to shift supplies. Once Benghazi and Tobruk were in Rommel's hands the cities also became depots for thousands of tons of supplies and food. Interestingly the man on the left, while wearing tropical Luftwaffe trousers, seems to be sporting a black Panzertruppen jacket.

Above: German ships ablaze in Tripoli harbour. Rommel's adjutant Major Hans-Joachim Schraepler noted in early May 1941, 'Tripoli is regularly bombed and the entrance to its port mined. … In addition, there are losses of ships while crossing between Italy and Tripoli, and into the port of Tripoli.'

Below: German personnel examine a smashed and mangled transport ship in Tripoli harbour. During late February 1941 a British submarine sank a ship on its return journey, while a hospital ship was sunk outside the entrance to Tripoli harbour by a mine. Craft sent up the coast to Benghazi were also attacked.

Opposite above: Italian soldiers view the damage on Tripoli's quayside; the vessel has lost its stern and the berth is rendered inoperable. Major Schraepler was dismissive of their defensive efforts, remarking, 'The Italians don't do anything. They have no planes and no fleet to fight in the Mediterranean. It is depressing.' This was not entirely true, but the Italian Navy, lacking carriers and radar, regularly avoided giving battle.

Opposite below: An Italian soldier half-heartedly sweeps debris into the harbour. The fate of the vessel behind him illustrates Field Marshal Kesselring's concerns that the handling of shipping in Tripoli harbour was simply too slow.

Germans watch from a rooftop the results of an air raid. The RAF and the combined Desert Air Force, which included the Australians and South Africans, constantly took the initiative, first taking the war to the Italians and then the Germans.

German supply columns going in both directions on the Via Balbia. 'The main road', observed Rommel, 'is a sea of pot-holes with the amount of traffic on it.'

Opposite inset: The Via Balbia along the North African coast was horribly exposed and regularly subjected to air attack. Major Schraepler reported that 'Transport by road is time consuming and costs material.'

Above inset: Trucks on the open desert road. Rommel wrote to his wife on 26 March 1942 complaining, 'Supply difficulties, particularly getting the stuff up overland, are still a great headache.'

Beyond the Via Balbia, the interior roads such as those up in the Jebel Akhdar were atrocious. The villages were connected by little more than dirt tracks, which were often unsuitable for wheeled vehicles. The Jebel Akhdar is also the wettest area of the whole of Libya.

A German column transporting fuel or water. The second truck is towing a double trailer. Most German divisions were backed by motorised supply battalions. For the 5th Light Division the supply battalions were the 533rd and 619th. These included light, heavy, water and fuel supply columns.

Securing water was vital, which meant controlling the oases and wells. Major Schraepler observed, 'From farmer to farmer or from water source to water source the distances are impressive.'

A very welcome sight – fresh water pouring from a well. Units such as the 641st and 645th Motorised Water Columns belonging to the 5th Light Division struggled to get adequate quantities of water forward. By May 1942 Rommel and his men were reduced to half a cup of water a day.

Above left: Donkey power. This method of drawing water from the deep well was hardly high-tech. The Germans could have deployed a pump but that required a regular flow of petrol and maintenance; donkeys were much less demanding.

Above right: Here a pipeline has been laid across the desert to create a filling station. 'A soldier arriving in a desert immediately adapts himself psychologically to the expected lack of water,' observed Colonel Fritz Bayerlein, Rommel's Chief of Staff.

Opposite: Water being siphoned into jerrycans from a bowser. The special filling rack could hold a dozen jerrycans at once. The worn white crosses on them indicated that they were for water only.

German vehicles, when they could, kept well spaced out on the long exposed road to avoid air attack. The trees offered little in the way of cover.

Above: Driving past rows of fruit or olive trees, the photographer could not resist taking a quick snap out of his moving vehicle.

This is what greeted the Axis supply columns out in the desert. 'Heat and lots of dust,' remarked Rommel. The dust regularly drew unwanted attention from enemy aircraft and artillery.

A German supply truck stands idle while its crew take a break. For the month of March 1942 Panzer Army Afrika needed 60,000 tons of supplies but only received 18,000 tons.

Above: The crew of this Ju 52 enjoy a relaxed picnic beneath the wing of their aircraft. The cargo was cable drums; the cabling may have been destined for use with field telephones. During the spring of 1942 the Luftwaffe gained air superiority over the Mediterranean, having temporarily neutralised Malta. This allowed for an increased flow of material to Tripoli, Benghazi and Derna by ship.

Below: The only other way of getting troops and supplies forward was by using the Junkers Ju 52 transport aircraft. In April 1941 when units of the 15th Panzer Division arrived in Tripoli, Rommel had its rifle regiments flown to Derna airfield to support the 5th Light Division's attack on Tobruk.

9 Rest and Recreation

AXIS FORCES IN NORTH AFRICA were not constantly in combat. Many of the rear echelon units rarely saw action unless in danger of being overrun. German soldiers and their Italian allies liked to go to the cinema, shopping, souvenir hunting and swimming in the sea when on furlough. The Deutsches Soldatenkino Bengasi or the German Soldiers' Cinema Benghazi proved a popular draw where the men could relax for a few hours. Many counted the days until they would be granted leave and could fly home to see family and loved ones, or even get married.

An excellent group photo showing war correspondent Fritz Moosmüller larking about with members of the German 90th Light Division in Tunisia. Not a single piece of their clothing matches in colour. Their relaxed air suggests they are a safe distance from the front. This division, consisting of three infantry regiments, was commanded by Brigadier Carl-Hans Lungerhausen at the battle of El Alamein.

Above: A taste of home. Bratwurst, bread and schnapps for lunch. Clearly this photograph was not intended for publication. Moosmüller's correspondent/reporter collar tabs are clearly visible.

Below: Perhaps a little inebriated, the men doze contentedly in the sun, using their greatcoats as improvised blankets. Their uniforms are conspicuously a very grubby white. The nearest has the silver Panzer Assault Badge pinned to his breast pocket, which means he has taken part in three tank actions on three different days. The Afrika Korps cuff title is just visible on his coat sleeve to the left.

Opposite: Sheltering from the sun, this soldier enjoys grapes straight from the vine. North Africa had been making wine since at least Roman times.

Below: The opportunity to prepare a hot meal was always welcome. The cook is undoubtedly looking forward to sharing the crate of Italian Birra Wührer to his right with his comrades. Warm beer was presumably better than no beer.

German troops strolling in an Arab bazaar. The man walking towards the camera is from a Luftwaffe flak unit. To his left is an Italian soldier, rifle slung across his back, keeping the peace.

Another member of the Luftwaffe out shopping. He seems to be interested in the two Libyan colonial soldiers to his left wearing red tarbushes. One is facing him, the other has his back turned. Beyond the group in the middle, both behind them and to their right, are Italian soldiers also out shopping. None of them carries firearms, so they are off duty.

A baker and his two sons sell a German soldier freshly made flatbread. The boy on his right seems to enjoy having his picture taken.

Chow interrupted. Staff of at a Luftwaffe field post office examine leather wallets brought in by a local trader. It is not clear what all the other items are laid out on the floor. The potential buyer is wearing a white *Bergmütze*, while his colleague to the left is in a sand-coloured *Feldmütze*. The buyer, as well as examining two wallets, is also holding his mess tin. The soldier on the right is wearing plimsolls that were popular with motorised troops and is also holding his mess tin and a spoon. The field post box is marked '3 Staffel' or 3rd Squadron.

Above: Everyone launches into a bit of good-natured haggling, while the man in the middle decides it is a good time for a cigarette.

Opposite: Fritz Moosmüller acting like a tourist sightseeing among the extensive Roman ruins. The Iron Cross First Class is pinned to his left breast pocket.

More Roman ruins, more German tourists. It is hard to imagine there was a war going on.

German troops enjoying the opportunity to bathe in the Mediterranean. The sea was the scene of numerous bloody naval battles between the Axis fleets and the Royal Navy, but it remained a place of recreation for the armies on both sides. The bathers have all neatly bundled their uniforms.

Above: Where is the sun tan lotion? The man on the left is either newly in-country or has not taken off his uniform for some considerable time. The whiteness of his face suggests the former rather than the latter. His older comrade has more of a tan.

Opposite: The ultimate goal of all Germans serving in North Africa: leave to return home. A smiling Fritz Moosmüller poses happily with his wife. Looking every inch the North Africa veteran, his tunic is suitably sun bleached and washed out. He is wearing the maligned jodhpurs and desert boots, which give him a rather dashing air. He is also sporting the Iron Cross, First and Second Class.

Above: This shot was taken on a different day as Moosmüller is wearing brown baggy tropical trousers pulled down over his desert boots. These had drawstrings to pull them tight on the ankle. Such tastes of home were always fleeting and were made bitter-sweet when returning to active duty.

Right: One last family photo before flying back to North Africa.

Opposite: Moosmüller out walking with family members and his young son.

Moosmüller, on the left, back in Tunisia ready to chronicle the Axis' final defence. Lieutenant Heinz Werner Schmidt, who went on to write his memoir *With Rommel in the Desert*, was extremely lucky as he flew home on leave to get married just two weeks before the German surrender in Tunisia.

Part Four

War in the Skies

10 Seaplane to Tripoli

THE LUFTWAFFE EMPLOYED A large variety of seaplanes in the Mediterranean, including the Blohm and Voss Bv 222 Wiking and Dornier Do 24 flying-boats as well as the Arado Ar 196 and Heinkel He 59 coastal reconnaissance floatplanes. The Regia Aeronautica and the Regia Marina also deployed flying-boats and floatplanes, principally the CRDA Cant Z.501 Gabbiano and the CRDA Cant Z.506. Luftwaffe Field Marshal Albert Kesselring recalled in his memoirs, 'All German aircraft flew with extra tanks, all air–sea-rescue aircraft were kept ready for take-off and rescue ships ready to put to sea or at their stations.'

Above: The Dornier Do 24 flying-boat was originally designed for the Dutch Navy for use in the East Indies. After the war broke out it was deployed by the Luftwaffe and built in Germany as well as in the occupied Netherlands and France. To the embarrassment of the pilot, this Do 24 somehow hit Tripoli's harbour wall in 1942. The left-hand engine has struck the building; this means that the lower wing, which was forward of the upper, was damaged.

Main image: Rear view of the same aircraft, showing the rather prominent tail turret armed with a 7.92mm machine gun. Lift was provided by the three engines on the upper wings.

The Do 24's power-operated dorsal turret, visible to the left of the crew, was armed with a 20mm MG 151 cannon. The bow also featured a turret armed with a 7.92mm machine gun that was in front of the cockpit and the pilot's line of vision. The crew are all wearing the Luftwaffe's lightweight tropical uniform.

A Do 24 in Tripoli harbour, 1942. The crew are in a mixture of sand and white tropical uniform. The officer appears to have injured his finger while helping to load the aircraft. This aircraft type acted in a maritime patrol role as well as search and rescue so was a welcome sight for downed aircrew.

Rear view of a Heinkel He 59 coastal reconnaissance floatplane moored off Tripoli harbour. This twin-engine biplane first appeared in the early 1930s and could also be used as a bomber as it could carry a 2,205lb bomb load or a single torpedo. The He 59 first saw combat with the German Condor Legion during the Spanish Civil War, when it was employed in anti-shipping patrols and for night bombing. In the Mediterranean it was used for air–sea rescue and a few conducted mine-laying operations. Sunken Italian freighters can be seen on the left.

This Luftwaffe officer was photographed outside his headquarters in Tripoli in 1942. He served as a reconnaissance pilot for a He 59 floatplane. Interestingly, he is still wearing his standard European Luftwaffe uniform, which indicates he is newly arrived.

It is unclear why this Italian CRDA Cant Z.506 reconnaissance/bomber floatplane is being transported on some sort of barge. Initially in the 1930s this type of aircraft had been used as an airliner flying wealthy Italians around the Mediterranean. In particular, rich businessmen needed a way to get to the opulent Grand Hotel Tripoli and the Uaddan Hotel and Casino. The military version known as the Z.506B Airone (Heron) appeared in 1937. The tail of this aircraft is clearly sporting the Italian Air Force's white cross.

The biggest operational flying-boat during the Second World War was the very rare Blohm and Voss Bv 222 Wiking. Only about a dozen were ever built. Intended for Lufthansa for flights to New York, this massive aircraft was powered by six engines. The prototype V1 after initial operations in Norway was transferred to the Mediterranean, where it was used to support the German war effort in North Africa. This V6 Wiking is floating in the waters off Tripoli in 1942.

The V6, having delivered its cargo, commences taxiing. It was important for the pilot to get away as quickly as possible. The Wiking could carry up to 18,000kg of freight or seventy-six fully equipped troops.

The mighty Wiking in a shower of spray starts its take-off run. The V6 and V8 were shot down by RAF Beaufighters while flying from Taranto in Italy to Tripoli in August and December 1942 respectively. The V8 had been operational for less than two months. The V1 served in the Mediterranean until February 1943, when it hit a wreck while landing at Piraeus harbour and sank.

11 Tri-motor Workhorse

THE LUFTWAFFE'S WORKHORSE FOR airborne and supply duties was the Junkers Ju 52/3m tri-motor medium bomber and troop transport. It was particularly effective in North Africa where it was regularly used to move men, equipment and fuel for both the Army and the Luftwaffe. Bf 109 and Bf 110 as well as Ju 87 pilots operating from forward airfields far out in the desert were always glad to see the Ju 52 approaching. It was dubbed 'Tante Ju' – 'Aunt Ju' or 'Auntie'. Thanks to its appearance it was also known rather unflatteringly as 'Iron Annie'.

Most of the Ju 52s operating in the Mediterranean and North Africa seem to have retained their standard Luftwaffe green paint scheme. Those involved in Operation *Mercury* and the invasion of Crete did use various camouflage patterns. The crew of this aircraft are working on the dorsal gun position, which was armed with a 7.92mm MG 15 machine gun. A side machine gun is also visible. The aircraft had a retractable ventral gun position. The bodywork was very distinctive, with its markedly corrugated skin.

This example of the Luftwaffe's Ju 52 tri-motor workhorse carries the name *Narvik* and was presumably a veteran of the 1940 Norway campaign. The Ju 52 also saw large-scale action in the Low Countries and Crete. The man standing beneath is Luftwaffe war correspondent Otto Vieth.

Time for a quick snack. Photographed by Otto Vieth, these men are wearing a variety of tropical uniform. The flying officer in the middle is attired in short-sleeved tropical shirt with chest pockets and shorts with turn-ups. He has a white tropical field cap, a design that was formalised as the *Einheitsfeldmütze* in 1943. In his arm is a military-issue water bottle.

The man in the middle has decided it would be humorous not to cooperate with Otto Vieth. He has brown leather desert boots with the socks rolled down, presumably to help keep the sand out. His colleagues are dressed in tropical long-sleeved shirts and baggy full-length trousers. Note the large thigh pocket.

Above: The trio finally agreed to pose for Vieth, but even then the man on the right is looking off into the distance. The dorsal gun position was open to the elements and the only protection for the gunner was the forward-facing windscreen, which can be seen behind the men.

Below: It is Otto Vieth's turn to pose for the camera, seated in the dorsal gun position.

This 'Aunt Ju', with its engines running, is taxiing for take-off. The large fixed flaps running the length of the wings reduced the landing speed, which meant the aircraft could operate from small airfields. This capability was particularly useful when using temporary airstrips to resupply troops at the front. The ground crews were sometimes not as diligent as they should have been in clearing rocks and other desert debris, which meant take-off and landing could be a bone-shaking experience.

Once airborne the Ju 52 had an economical cruising speed of 130mph or 210kmh. It could carry almost 5,000kg, double its own weight, to a range of 800 miles using auxiliary fuel tanks.

The Ju 52 suffered very heavy losses during Operation *Mercury* in May 1941, with hundreds of transports destroyed or seriously damaged. Afterwards Hitler vowed never to conduct any further large-scale paratroop operations.

Another fine photograph by Otto Vieth showing an 'Auntie' skimming over the still waters of the Mediterranean. The aircraft could carry eighteen troops, or twelve casualty litters, or freight. Once the RAF began to operate from Malta in growing numbers such flights from Sicily became much more hazardous.

The Ju 52's maximum speed was 170mph or 275kmh, which left it very vulnerable to attack. In North Africa the Luftwaffe's transport squadrons regularly received a mauling by the Allied Desert Air Force. On one occasion on 18 April 1943 about 100 'Aunties' were shot down in a single day.

Above: The colour in this image very clearly shows how the German transport fleet was pushed to its limits. Both aircraft are filthy and rusty. The paint has been scoured by the desert and the nearest aircraft has rust streaks trailing back from the engine, caused by condensation as well as oil staining from the engine. Ground crews had to work day and night to keep such aircraft airworthy.

Opposite: Vieth has caught the tired expressions of this aircrew, safely back on the ground. Hermann Meyer (seated in the doorway) is wearing the unique Luftwaffe tropical peak cap. This featured a neck-flap similar to that on the French Foreign Legion kepi to give added protection from the sun. After saving trapped German divisions at Kholm and Demyansk on the Eastern Front, Hitler thought his transport aircraft could sustain the German Army trapped at Stalingrad. In the face of the reinvigorated Red Air Force they failed, with heavy losses. Hitler also insisted the 'Auntie' and other transport aircraft ferry troops and equipment into Tunisia in late 1942.

12 Desert Aviation

THE LUFTWAFFE ARRIVED IN the Mediterranean long before the Afrika Korps. In December 1940 Hitler deployed the 10th Air Corps to Sicily to support the Italian Regia Aeronautica and to attack British shipping. Its inventory included the Ju-87 dive-bomber, Ju 88 medium bomber and the Bf 109 fighter. On 3 February 1941 Hitler ordered the 10th Air Corps to attack the British in Cyrenaica, which clearly signalled he had no intention of abandoning Mussolini. Once Rommel's forces began to arrive, Luftwaffe units were sent to support him. The 8th Air Corps was then deployed to assist in the German invasion of Crete, which involved two divisions transported by the 11th Air Corps. The 2nd Air Corps was sent to Sicily to bomb the British garrison on Malta into surrendering.

Above: The Fieseler Fi 156 Storch (Stork) reconnaissance aircraft was a common sight in North Africa and was regularly used by Rommel as a liaison aircraft. This one is from the C-Series. Its large glazed cabin provided good visibility for its three-man crew. The Storch gained its name courtesy of its stork-leg-like undercarriage. It needed only about 200ft (60m) to take off and just a third of that to land. This short take-off and landing capability made it well suited to the rough desert conditions. Known as a 'go-anywhere' aircraft, around 2,550 were built during the Second World War. The Storch was widely used by other Axis countries, including Italy. It was also built in occupied France and Czechoslovakia. Its low speed, however, meant that it was vulnerable to ground fire and enemy fighters.

Opposite: This Luftwaffe lieutenant is wearing a decidedly relaxed-looking tropical uniform, far more comfortable and practical than that issued to the Army. His white short-sleeved shirt is adorned with the distinctive officer's Luftwaffe breast eagle. The single pip and lack of braid on his shoulder tabs show that he is a junior officer. The corps colours or *Waffenfarben* on his tabs are an indistinct purple, making him potentially either military judiciary or a field chaplain.

Above: The Fi 156C had a raised rear cabin that allowed for a rear-firing 7.92mm machine gun. The Fi 156C-1 was deployed for liaison and staff transport duties, while the Fi 156C-2 was the reconnaissance variant equipped with a single camera (the 156-C5 carried the camera under the fuselage). Some of the C-2s were also used for casualty evacuation. The Fi 156C-3 was multi-role. Tropical versions of the C-3 and C-5 were fitted with engine sand filters. Rommel wrote on 8 April 1941 of a near miss while flying in one: 'The Italians had apparently never seen a Storch before and were so completely bewildered by our sudden appearance over their heads that they fired on us from all directions.'

Below: The Messerschmitt Bf 109 formed the mainstay of the Luftwaffe's fighter units in North Africa. Although better than the RAF's Hurricane and Tomahawk, it was never available in sufficient numbers. Once Rommel had driven the British from Cyrenaica, the Bf 109s and Ju 97s were able to support the Afrika Korps, flying from Derna and Gazala west of Tobruk. This Bf 109G was captured in Tunisia in May 1943 and its upper fuselage has neither the desert sand nor the desert camouflage scheme developed in North Africa.

Above: Rommel used the tropical version of the Junkers Ju 87 dive-bomber as flying artillery in North Africa. The two main variants deployed were the Ju 87B-2/Trop and the Ju 87D-1/Trop. The latter had a slightly different appearance and increased armour. From the shape of the cockpit, these aircraft are the earlier B-2 variant. By the summer of 1941 the Luftwaffe had deployed a Ju 87 Gruppe to Tripoli and a second one to Sirte.

Opposite: The Henschel Hs 126 short-range reconnaissance plane was built in the late 1930s. It could be deployed for photographic missions using a handheld camera in the rear cockpit, supplemented by a Zeiss camera in the rear fuselage. Armament comprised one forward-firing 7.92mm MG 17 machine gun plus another one on a movable mount in the rear cockpit. For bombing missions, it could carry a single 110lb bomb or five 22lb bombs. The Hs 126 was relatively rare as only 600 were built and it was phased out of front-line service in 1942, being replaced by the Focke-Wulf Fw 189. Before Hitler's invasion of Greece, the Greek Air Force purchased sixteen Hs 126. The man posing beneath this aircraft may be an Afrika Korps intelligence or liaison officer.

This Junkers Ju 88 bomber operating against Malta only just made it back to Sicily in March 1941, where it conducted a wheels-up landing. Apart from the bent propeller props, it has suffered damage to the nose and cockpit. Mount Etna is in the background, the scene of stubborn German resistance in the summer of 1943. This type was the Luftwaffe's most versatile aircraft of the war and remained in production throughout. In the summer of 1941 a Ju 88 Geschwader was deployed to Benghazi to support Rommel and the Afrika Korps.

Above: This Luftwaffe captain is enjoying a breakfast of sausage, toast and coffee while perusing the newspapers. A special staff known as the Luftgaustab zbV Afrika was formed in 1941 to oversee the ground organisation of the Luftwaffe and its supply routes. This was also responsible for the flak units protecting the airfields, harbours and supply bases.

Opposite: Major Heinrich Bindewald photographed in Sicily while serving with the 2nd Fliegergruppe in 1943. The previous year he had been on the Eastern Front with the 2nd Luftwaffe Field Division in the Minsk area. His tropical uniform shows a mix of colours, with his tunic looking almost pink in the sunlight.

Luftwaffe officers relaxing in the sun and watching flying displays over the Mediterranean. Most of them are wearing short-sleeved shirts and shorts. Some have side caps on and a few are wearing white 'crusher' style caps. The man in the foreground with his back to the camera has clearly just arrived as he is still in his European theatre blue-grey uniform, the matching peak cap can be seen on the wall to the right of him.

Below: Larking about and laughter for the camera. The Luftwaffe ground strength in North Africa reached 12,000 men and 3,400 vehicles by September 1942. However, the Mediterranean was not considered a Luftwaffe priority and did not receive the same scale of resources used on the Eastern Front or in the defence of Germany.

Above: Where it could, the Luftwaffe co-opted Italian facilities for its own use. The hangar and concrete accommodation blocks would have made ideal homes for Luftwaffe units deployed to North Africa when not flying in support of the Afrika Korps. Apart from their air bases in Sicily and southern Italy, the Regia Aeronautica's main facilities in Libya were at Tripoli, Benghazi and Tobruk. Its forward airfields in the Tobruk area were to the south and south-east of the port, located at El Adem, Gambut and Sid Rezegh. As the war flowed back and forth these airfields became hotly contested.

The results of an Allied air attack leave columns of black smoke rising on the horizon. A number of aircraft can be seen exposed on the airfield. It is not clear what the men in the foreground are doing.

The detail of this Luftwaffe aircraft is rather indistinct, but looks very similar to the Italian Caprioni Ca 314 patrol aircraft. The Germans were known for requisitioning all sorts of Italian equipment and it is possible that they repurposed this aircraft for transport duties. Alternately it may be a decoy to distract Allied bomber attacks.

The Allied air forces did not have things all their own way. German sightseers stop to examine a United States Army Air Force Curtiss P-40 Tomahawk fighter-bomber. Their vehicles, comprising a Kübelwagen and a Horch, are parked on the other side of the road. This aircraft appears to have crash-landed then been stripped by eager souvenir hunters. The Germans are wearing brown greatcoats, reed-green trousers, boots and light-grey field caps.

114

P-40Fs were flown from US carriers during Operation *Torch* in November 1942, which saw an Anglo-American invasion of Morocco and Algeria. The aircraft has a number of bullet holes.

Part Five

The Rise and Fall of the Deutsches Afrika Korps

13 Rommel Up Close

ERWIN ROMMEL, AFTER THE French campaign in 1940, rose from being a divisional commander, to corps commander, to army commander and finally to the commander of an army group. Hitler on 22 June 1942 promoted him to field marshal as a reward for his decisive victory at Tobruk. Rommel wrote to his wife that he would much rather have received another division of troops. The victory at Tobruk came at a price. Although his men only suffered 3,360 casualties, some 15 per cent of his force, the toll included 300 officers, which was 70 per cent of his commanders. At the time of his promotion, he was so preoccupied that he failed to change his shoulder badges to the two crossed batons denoting a field marshal. Kesselring reminded him when he reached El Alamein and gave Rommel a pair of his own badges.

A fine portrait of Rommel and his staff. The composition is so good that it is hard to know if this was posed. Rommel's very white forehead shows that he was rarely without a hat. Knight's Cross winner Fritz Bayerlein is in the centre. The stooping colonel on the left is using a field telephone to disseminate Rommel's latest orders.

A Nazi propaganda coup. South African prisoners being marched back towards Tobruk after the garrison surrendered. It consisted of the 2nd South African Division under Major General Hendrik Klopper plus supporting British and Indian brigades. Rommel captured almost 33,000 troops, making it the second-largest British capitulation after Singapore. Rommel's finest moments were at Mechili, Gazala and Tobruk, though it took him fourteen months to capture the latter. At Gazala he took 6,000 prisoners.

The prisoners reach Tobruk. Some 2,000 tons of petrol, 5,000 tons of food and 2,000 serviceable vehicles fell into Rommel's hands along with large quantities of ammunition. The capture of the port meant that German plans to invade Malta were shelved; it also encouraged Rommel's drive on the Nile and ultimate defeat at El Alamein.

Rommel once again in conference. From left to right: Siegfried Westphal, Wilhelm Ritter von Thoma, Fritz Bayerlein, then Rommel. The complete lack of uniformity among his officers in North Africa is very evident here. They dressed for comfort rather than smartness. True to form, Rommel has struck a pose for the photographer that is mirrored by those around him.

An orderly offers a very tired-looking Rommel hot coffee. Rommel lived a Spartan existence in North Africa, eschewing any luxuries. This inevitably had a detrimental effect on his health. In 1938 when he was director of the military school at Wiener Neustadt, he told the cadets, 'Never spare yourself, and let the troops see that you don't, in your endurance of fatigue and privation.'

Holding his coffee cup very tightly, the Field Marshal appears to be telling off General Wilhelm Ritter von Thoma for some perceived failure. Rommel was not always the easiest man to work for and was hard on himself and those around him. Rommel's advice in such situations was, 'Always be tactful … Avoid excessive sharpness or harshness of voice …'

Trophy of war. While Rommel scans the battlefield his staff examine an American-built M3 Stuart light tank. During Operation *Crusader* in November 1941 the British had 163 of these in service, making it the very first American tank to see combat with the British 8th Army. The 'HQ' on the turret marks this as a headquarters tank.

HQ
T.28059

Rommel indulging in a rare break from command, sightseeing in Sicily in 1942. He disliked being away from the front as it meant he had to indulge in the politics of command involving Field Marshal Albert Kesselring and the Italians.

Rommel visible on the right peering from the roof of his captured Mammoth armoured command vehicle. Tragically Major Hans-Joachim Schraepler met his end on 9 December 1941 thanks to it. Later Rommel sadly wrote home to his wife, 'I don't think I've told you yet that Schraepler met with a fatal accident (run over by the Mammoth).'

Caught in an unguarded moment, Rommel turns to scowl at the cameraman, Fritz Moosmüller, perhaps tired of the constant intrusion.

The Field Marshal inspecting German positions in Tunisia. He was unhappy at Hitler's instance that the Axis armies fight on in North Africa and felt they should have been evacuated to Sicily. PK-reporter Fritz Moosmüller with beard is winding film in one of his two Leica cameras in the foreground.

The dashing panzer commander. This is how the German public saw Field Marshal Rommel. At the collar he is wearing the Knight's Cross and just visible beneath it the Pour le Mérite. Nazi propaganda was so effective that he and his men were inundated with letters requesting signed photos and women seeking pen pals. He was understandably dismayed when Hitler refused to allow him to remain with his troops in Tunisia. Instead he would orchestrate the occupation of northern Italy in the summer of 1943 and the installation of a puppet regime nominally under Mussolini.

14 Defeat in Tunisia

HITLER, FOLLOWING THE ANGLO-AMERICAN landings in French Algeria and Morocco on 8 November 1942, was determined not to abandon his campaign in North Africa. Catching the Allies by surprise, the Luftwaffe rapidly flew some 40,000 troops and 14,000 tons of supplies into Tunis. Another 50,000 men arrived by sea. These forces easily overwhelmed the 15,000 French troops in Tunisia. They then secured Rommel's rear and ensured the Germans kept fighting in North Africa until 12 May 1943.

Once the Axis forces were cornered in Tunisia, defeat became only a matter of time. Hitler, disastrously for the Axis, refused to authorise an evacuation to Sicily, which resulted in 125,000 German and 115,000 Italian soldiers being trapped. Among them were the original divisions of the Afrika Korps. 'My father's consolation was that the troops', recalled Manfred Rommel, 'which he had sadly seen surrender at the capitulation of Tunis were spared – as prisoners of war – from being senselessly sacrificed in the final battles which Hitler had ordered.'

German troops began to arrive in force by air in Tunis on 9 November 1942 just a day after the Allied landings in Morocco and Algeria. The crew of this Ju 52 were expecting trouble as the gunner can be seen in the dorsal position and the pilot is flying low in the hope of avoiding being spotted by enemy fighters.

Ju 52s ferrying German troops from Sicily to Tunisia. French Air Force airfields around Tunis and Bizerte were quickly seized to facilitate the occupation. Part of the French garrison remained loyal to the Vichy government and did nothing to prevent the German takeover.

Above: Among the aircraft employed to help with the Axis occupation of Tunisia was the mighty Messerschmitt Me 323 Gigant (Giant) heavy general-purpose transport. Its size and six engines enabled it to carry 15,000kg of cargo. These Luftwaffe personnel are unloading a Horch staff car belonging to the German Army. The pilot, in officer's cap, is standing to the left looking at the camera.

Opposite: The aircraft's cargo included a Sd Kfz 11 3-ton half-track, which appears freshly sprayed sand colour. The loading ramp is decidedly too short for the vehicle. The aircraft's cockpit is located just above the open bow doors.

For the return flight this Me 323 is being loaded with Me 109 engines in need of overhaul. At first the Me 323, flying alongside the Ju 52 in fleets of up to 100 aircraft with fighter escort, operated largely unscathed. However, the Me 323's inability to take evasive action meant this soon began to change. In mid-April 1943, from a flight of sixteen aircraft just two survived attack by the RAF, the rest went down in the Mediterranean.

Below: This particular Me 323 was destroyed on the ground. The side gunner positions have surprisingly remained largely intact and the machine guns are still in their mounts.

Above: While the skeleton of the tail and wings remain, the front section has vanished. As three of the engines are facing the aircraft it may have been that they were removed for maintenance. A Ju 52 can just be seen in the middle ground on the right. After the Axis surrender in Tunisia, the remaining Me 323s were deployed to the Eastern Front, where they operated behind the front line.

Below: Al-Zaytuna or Ez-Zitouna mosque, Tunis 1942. Once in the city the Germans swiftly secured the full cooperation of Admiral Jean-Pierre Esteva, the senior French official in Tunisia. General Georges Barré, the French ground forces commander, sided with the Allies and withdrew westwards to link up with them. After the war Esteva was tried and found guilty of treason.

Above: Kriegsberichter Fritz Moosmüller looking out over Tunisia. He would chart the German build-up and the subsequent defeat of 5th Panzer Army.

Moosmüller and a colleague enjoy a glass of wine as if on holiday in the French Riviera. It is hard to believe that to the west and the south Axis forces would soon be fighting desperately to maintain Hitler's last foothold in North Africa. After abandoning Tripoli in January 1943, Rommel successfully withdrew to the Mareth Line on the Libyan–Tunisian border.

Opposite inset: The Germans were treated to a parade by this French colonial cavalry regiment, smartly turned out despite their lack of horses. The troopers' full dress includes a black tunic without epaulettes and elongated Austrian knots in red. The red fez and black tunic are very similar to those worn by Zouave infantry regiments, which were solely recruited from Frenchmen in North Africa.

Above: The parade included full military honours with a large marching band. The colour party comprises Zouaves in the 1927-issue 'oriental' full dress. The Germans must have been amused by such pomp when a war was going on.

Opposite: This Tunisian Spahi light cavalryman, photographed by Fritz Moosmüller, has retained his horse. Algeria, Morocco and Tunisia all had French colonial Spahi regiments. He has two *bournous* or cloaks, which are blue and red.

Moosmüller, after photographing the Spahi unit, could not resist having a go. The *bournous* is a traditional Berber garment and was incorporated into the French Army of Africa's Spahi cavalry regiments. To his amusement Rommel was given one on arrival in North Africa. Writing to his wife on 26 March 1941, he recorded, 'Yesterday an Italian General, … made me a present of a bournous. It's a magnificent thing – blue-black with red silk and embroidery. It would do well for you as a theatre cloak.'

Above: Members of the German Propaganda Companies came across some peculiar units in Tunisia. Among them was the Légion des Voluntaires Français en Tunisie, also known as the Phalange Africaine, and the Deutsch-Arabische Truppen which briefly served the Axis. These German and Arab troops are marching under the Tunisian flag. On the whole, belated German attempts to appeal to Arab nationalism failed miserably.

Opposite: At least one battalion of Deutsch-Arabische Truppen was formed by Sonderverband 287 drawn from members of the German commando Brandenburg Division. These two German officers are in standard German tropical kit, while the Tunisian flag bearer is wearing a pre-war French Army uniform and French webbing with the 1916-pattern ammunition pouches.

Above: Apart from the German officer on the right, the only indication that these Tunisian volunteers are part of the German armed forces is the German helmet and a white armband stating 'Im Dienst der Deutsche Wehrmacht'. There were five battalions of Tunisians with the 5th Panzer Army, including those from the Phalange Africaine and Sonderverband 287. The presence of the horses and carts shows the unit was not motorised.

Below: After Axis defeats at Mareth, Longstop and Tunis, this was the fate of many former members of the Afrika Korps – a patch of dry soil in North Africa.

German cemeteries in North Africa were always well tended, even at the end in Tunisia.

Above: Total Axis losses in North Africa amounted to about 620,000 men, of whom over a third were German. After the Axis surrender the Italian 1st Army and German 5th Panzer Army ceased to exist, although the latter was later reconstituted in Normandy in 1944.

Opposite: The epitome of a sun-kissed desert warfare veteran. This sergeant's dust-covered ear indicates that before the photograph was taken his face was protected by goggles and a scarf, both of which are around his neck. The man's field-grey cap contrasts with his brown tunic. The twin silver pips on his sand-blasted uniform suggest he is a senior staff sergeant. The golden-yellow *Waffenfarben* shows he was serving with a reconnaissance unit. Rommel's adventures with the Deutsches Afrika Korps had first started with the 3rd Reconnaissance Battalion back in February 1941.

Deutsches Afrika Korps Order of Battle

Operation *Sunflower*, February–April 1941
DAK: Generalleutnant Erwin Rommel

5th Light Division (from 1 August 1941 21st Panzer Division): Generalmajor Johannes Streich (23 July 1941 replaced by Generalleutnant Johann von Ravenstein)
5th Panzer Regiment: 1st and 2nd Panzer Battalions
200th Rifle Regiment: 2nd and 8th (Motorised) Machine Gun Battalions, plus the 3rd Reconnaissance Battalion
1st Battalion, 33rd Flak Regiment
1st Battalion, 75th Artillery Regiment
39th (Motorised) Panzerjäger Battalion
605th Panzerjäger Battalion
606th Self-propelled Flak Battalion

Engaged against Operation *Battleaxe*, June 1941
DAK: Generalleutnant Erwin Rommel

Corps Troops:
Two Italian artillery regiments in Bardia
One German 88mm flak regiment

5th Light Division: Generalleutnant Johann von Ravenstein
5th Panzer Regiment
3rd Reconnaissance Battalion

15th Panzer Division: Generalleutnant Walter Neumann-Silkow
8th Panzer Regiment
104th Rifle Regiment
33rd Reconnaissance Battalion
PaK anti-tank battery
88mm flak battery
Divisional artillery at Point 206

Trento Infantry Division
Three Italian infantry battalions and one artillery regiment

Engaged against Operation *Crusader*, November 1941
Commandante Superiore: Generale d'Armata Ettore Bastico

Panzer Group Afrika: General der Panzertruppen Erwin Rommel

DAK: Generalleutnant Ludwig Crüwell

15th Panzer Division: Generalleutnant Walter Neumann-Silkow (died of wounds 9 December 1941)
8th Panzer Regiment
15th Rifle Brigade
33rd Reconnaissance Battalion
Divisional artillery

21st Panzer Division: Generalleutnant Johann von Ravenstein (captured 29 November 1941)
5th Panzer Regiment
104th Rife Regiment
3rd Reconnaissance Battalion
Divisional artillery and engineers

Division zur besonderen Verwendung Afrika (zbV – from 27 November 1941 90th Light Division): Generalleutnant Max Sümmermann (died of wounds 10 December 1941)
155th Rifle Regiment
361st Afrika Regiment
288th Sonderverband
580th Reconnaissance Battalion
605th Panzerjäger Battalion

Savona 55th Infantry Division
Two infantry regiments and an artillery regiment

Engaged at El Alamein, July–November 1942
Commando Supremo Africa: Marshal Ettore Bastico

Panzer Army Afrika: Feldmarschall Erwin Rommel
DAK: Generalleutnant Wilhelm Ritter von Thoma

15th Panzer Division: Generalmajor Gustav von Vaerst
8th Panzer Regiment
115th Panzer Grenadier Regiment
33rd Artillery Regiment

33rd Anti-Tank Battalion
33rd Engineer Battalion

21st Panzer Division: Generalmajor Heinz von Randow
5th Panzer Regiment
104th Panzergrenadier Regiment
155th Artillery Regiment
39th Anti-Tank Battalion
200th Engineer Battalion

Other German units at El Alamein: 90th Light Division, 164th Afrika Light Division and Ramcke Parachute Brigade.

All four divisions ended their days with Army Group Afrika under the Italian 1st Army defending southern Tunisia. The 5th Panzer Army also part of Army Group Afrika, defending northern Tunisia, contained five German divisions including the 10th Panzer Division.

Sources and Further Reading

Atkinson, Rick. *An Army at Dawn: The War in North Africa 1942-1943*. London: Little, Brown, 2003.

Barnett, Correlli. *The Desert Generals*. London: Pan, 1983.

Buckingham, William F. *Tobruk: The Great Siege 1941–2*. Stroud: Tempus, 2008.

Butler, Daniel Allen. *Field Marshal: The Life and Death of Erwin Rommel*. Oxford: Casemate, 2015.

Carruthers, Bob (ed.). *The Afrika Korps in Combat*. Barnsley: Pen & Sword, 2013.

Carver, Michael. *Tobruk*. London: Pan, 1972.

Chamberlain, Peter & Doyle, Hilary. *Encyclopaedia of German Tanks of World War Two: The Complete Illustrated Directory of German Battle Tanks, Armoured Cars, Self-Propelled Guns and Semi-Tracked Vehicles, 1939–1945*. Wigston: Silverdale Books, 2004.

Church, John. *Military Vehicles of World War II*. Poole: Blandford Press, 1982.

Dimbleby, Jonathan. *Destiny in the Desert: The Road to El Alamein – The Battle that Turned the Tide*. London: Profile, 2013.

Ellis, Chris. *21st Panzer Division: Rommel's Afrika Korps Spearhead*. Hersham: Ian Allan, 2001.

Ford, Ken. *El Alamein 1942: The Turning of the Tide*. Oxford: Osprey, 2001.

Ford, Ken. *Operation Crusader 1941: Rommel in Retreat*. Oxford: Osprey, 2010.

Forty, George & Livesey, Jack. *The Complete Guide to Tanks and Armoured Fighting Vehicles*. London: Hermes House, 2006.

Forty, Jonathan. *Tanks in Detail: Pzkpfw IV Ausf A to J Panzer IV*. Hersham: Ian Allan, 2002.

Gander, Terry J. *Tanks in Detail: PzKpfw III Ausf A to N Panzer III*. Hersham: Ian Allan, 2004.

Gilbert, Adrian. *The Imperial War Museum Book of the Desert War*. London: Sidgwick and Jackson, 1995.

Gudmundsson, Bruce (ed.). *Inside the Afrika Korps: The Crusader Battles, 1941–1942*. Barnsley: Frontline, 2016.

Harrison. Frank. *Tobruk: The Great Siege Reassessed*. London: Brockhampton Press, 1999.

Hogg, Ian. *Twentieth-Century Artillery*. Hoo: Grange Books, 2005.

Holland, James. *Together We Stand: Turning the Tide in the West – North Africa 1942–1943*. London: HarperCollins, 2005.

Jurado, Carlos Caballero. *Foreign Volunteers of the Wehrmacht 1941–45*. London: Osprey, 1983.

Kershaw, Andrew & Close, Ian. *The Desert War*. London: Phoebus, 1975.

Kesselring, Albert. *The Memoirs of Field-Marshal Kesselring*. London: William Kimber, 1974.

Lewin, Ronald. *Rommel as Military Commander*. Barnsley: Pen & Sword, 2004.

Liddell Hart, B.H. (ed.). *The Rommel Papers*. London: Collins, 1953.

Lucas, James. *War in the Desert: The Eighth Army at El Alamein*. London: Arms and Armour Press, 1982.

Luck, Hans von. *Panzer Commander: The Memoirs of Colonel Hans von Luck*. London: Cassell, 2002.

Macksey, Kenneth. *Afrika Korps*. London: Pan/Ballantine, 1972.

Macksey, Kenneth. *Rommel Battles and Campaigns*. London: Arms and Armour Press, 1979.

Mellenthin, Major General F.W. von. *Panzer Battles*. London: Futura, 1984.

Mitchelhill-Green, David. *Rommel in North Africa: Quest for the Nile*. Barnsley: Pen & Sword, 2017.

Mollo, Andrew. *The Armed Forces of World War II: Uniforms, Insignia and Organization*. London: Black Cat, 1987.

Mollo, Andrew & Smith, Digby. *World Army Uniforms Since 1939*. Dorset: Blandford Press, 1986.

Mondey, David. *The Hamlyn Guide to Axis Aircraft of World War II*. London: Bounty Books, 2009.

Olive, Michael & Edwards, Robert. *Rommel's Desert Warriors 1941–42*. Barnsley: Pen & Sword, 2012.

Pitt, Barrie. *The Crucible of War: Western Desert 1941*. London: Futura, 1981.

Quarrie, Bruce. *Afrika Korps*. Cambridge: Patrick Stephens, 1975.

Sandars, John. *8th Army in the Desert*. Cambridge: Patrick Stephens, 1976.

Schmidt, Heinz Werner. *With Rommel in the Desert*. London: Panther, 1968.

Schraepler, Hans-Albrecht (ed.). *At Rommel's Side: The Lost Letters of Hans-Joachim Schraepler*. Barnsley: Frontline, 2009.

Stewart, Adrian. *Victory in the Desert*. London: Canelo, 2022.

Strawson, John. *The Battle for North Africa*. London: B.T. Batsford, 1969.

Thompson, Julian. *Forgotten Voices: Desert Victory*. London: Ebury Press, 2011.

Tucker-Jones, Anthony. *Armoured Warfare in the North African Campaign*. Barnsley: Pen & Sword, 2011.

Tucker-Jones, Anthony. *The Battle for the Mediterranean: Allied and Axis Campaigns from North Africa to the Italian Peninsula 1940–45*. London: Arcturus, 2021.

Tucker-Jones, Anthony. *The Desert Air War 1940–1943*. Barnsley: Pen & Sword, 2018.

Tute, Warren. *The North African War*. London: Sidgwick and Jackson, 1976.

Vanderveen, Bart. *Historic Military Vehicles Directory*. London: After the Battle, 1989.

Vanderveen, Bart. *The Observer's Fighting Vehicles Directory: World War II*. London: Frederick Warne, 1969.

Warner, Philip. *Alamein*. London: William Kimber, 1979.

Whiting, Charles. *First Blood: The Battle of Kasserine Pass*. London: Leo Cooper, 1984